LOOK TO

TO

D1474215

L
A
Z
A
R
U
S

THE BIG
STORE

David & Beverly Meyers
& Elise Meyers Walker

Charleston   London

THE
History
PRESS

Published by The History Press
Charleston, SC 29403
www.historypress.net

Cover design by Karleigh Hambrick.

First published 2011

Manufactured in the United States

ISBN 978.1.60949.299.1

Library of Congress Cataloging-in-Publication Data

Meyers, David, 1948-
Look to Lazarus : the big store / David and Beverly Meyers and Elise Meyers Walker.
p. cm.
Includes bibliographical references.
ISBN 978-1-60949-299-1
1. Lazarus Department Store 2. Department stores--United States--History. I. Meyers,
Beverly. II. Walker, Elise Meyers. III. Title.
HF5465.U64L39 2011
381'.1410973--dc23
2011033112

Notice: The information in this book is true and complete to the best of our knowledge. It is offered without guarantee on the part of the authors or The History Press. The authors and The History Press disclaim all liability in connection with the use of this book.

This book is dedicated to the memory of Virgil and Marie Meyers.

Contents

CONTENTS

Foreword

Our family was a Lazarus family. My dad did the selling, and my mom did the buying.

My father was Ben Hayes; in addition to being a popular columnist for the *Columbus Citizen* (later the *Citizen-Journal*), he sometimes wrote advertising copy for Lazarus and other businesses around town.

As a result, we were chosen to be the "poster family" for Lazarus's Father's Day advertising campaign in June 1953. The unabashedly silly photos were used to sell everything for father from "asbestos gloves" for the barbecue to the plastic revolving poker "Chip-O-Matic."

My mother, though depicted as a painter in the ads, was an accomplished seamstress. She and I spent much of our time in the fabric departments of Lazarus downtown. Both the bargain basement and the rarified atmosphere of the larger fifth-floor fabrics were my playground and second home.

I did like the toy department, especially dolls. You can bet that my mother made some fancy doll clothes. I still have the dolls and the clothes.

Once there was a TV special about two children, a boy and a girl, who were accidentally locked in Lazarus overnight. They played with the toys, yes, but they also jumped on the beds! I always wanted to jump on those beds.

I did try on the ladies' hats and sat in the easy chairs. The jewelry counter by the air curtain front door took up a lot of my time. And I loved to go to the Chintz Room and eat the nut bread. My mother got us all "dolled up" to go shopping, so we always had lunch downtown.

Writer Ben Hayes was the "star" of a special Father's Day advertising supplement in 1951. *CH.*

When I was in the Chintz Room with my father (he took his daughter to work before it was fashionable), we never got to eat lunch uninterrupted. People chatted with my dad constantly, giving him items for his column. At that time, my father may have been the most recognizable person in Columbus, along with his first cousin, Woody Hayes.

We had very long lunches. I ate slice after slice of nut bread. In addition to the human interest stories and gossip, my dad wrote about Columbus history. He never forgot a name or date. He was an amazing Columbus history raconteur. Sam Perdue, the former city editor of the *Citizen-Journal*, once said of him, "He had a fantastic and endless knowledge of Columbus."

I am so glad that David asked me to write this foreword. My dad would have loved this book. In fact, he would have written this book. He lamented and wrote about the loss of so many Columbus landmarks, including the people who made them. No one could have foreseen the loss of such an institution as the F&R Lazarus & Company, although, like its biblical namesake, the building rises again in a new configuration.

Foreword

I still have the Lazarus centennial commemorative plate, with six white carnations circling the three block buildings, the annex and the parking garage in the center, as well as all the former incarnations (pun intended) around the edge.

My mother always went to the foot of the escalator to shake "Mr. Lazarus's" hand. One of the brothers was often there to meet and greet.

A plate and the echo of a handshake. Doll clothes fabric. Old photos and ad copy. A nut bread recipe. And now this book in your hands. Lazarus, we loved you.

–Christine Hayes

Hayes is a columnist for the Short North Gazette. *Her columns, including "A Fortune in Fabric" and "Folded Copy Paper" (memoirs of her parents), can be found at shortnorth.com/Hayes.*

Acknowledgements

When History Press commissioning editor Joe Gartrell asked if we would be interested in doing a book on Lazarus, I said yes, but only if the family had no objections. Thanks to Kelly Budros, I was able to meet with Robert Lazarus Jr., the proverbial "last man standing" (in terms of the store, anyway). "Mr. Bob" graciously answered my questions and provided me with information that I might not otherwise have obtained. We wish to express our gratitude to him for his kindness and encouragement. (Hope he likes the book.)

As always, we are grateful to the good people at the Columbus Metropolitan Libraries, especially Julie Callahan and Nick Taggart. Without their assistance and encouragement, this book wouldn't be half as good. Jack Shaw and the other staff members who work the microfilm room also deserve a mention. Doing battle with those antiquated machines is a rather thankless job, so thanks!

British author Edgar Wallace once invited a friend to his estate for the weekend, only to disappear immediately after dinner on Friday evening. He wasn't seen again until Monday morning, when his friend learned that Wallace had occupied himself by dictating an eighty-thousand-word novel, *The Devil Man*, in less than sixty hours.

By contrast, it took us six months to research and write *Look to Lazarus: The Big Store*. Unlike Wallace, we did not have the luxury of being able to make things up (nor did we have use of his fabled "Plot Wheel"). For that reason, we are extremely appreciative of everyone who understood the time constraints and went out of their way to help us meet our deadline.

In no particular order, the roll of honor includes Leonard and Virginia Daloia, Betty Rosbottom, Dave Hundley, Christine Hayes (CH), Arnett Howard, Robert Stephenson (RS), Tara Narcross, Tom and Norma Eviston (TE), Karen Ross-Ohlinger (KRO), Jerry Bowling, Marilyn Shumaker Gerkins, Iris Cooper, Patricia Wilson (PW), Ed Hoffman (EH), Nick Pusecker, Leah Pusecker-Reynolds (LPR), Doug Motz, Sue Robenalt, Jennifer Hambrick (JH), Carie Davis, Alex Campbell, Dan Dow, Cynthia Robins, Tony Cox, Mary Lou Kunkler (MLK), Neil Morrison, Angela Lookabaugh, Randy Ketcham (RK), Jennifer Walker and Craig Holman. Initials in parenthesis indicate photo credits.

Additional photo credits include Columbus Metropolitan Library (CML), Grandview Heights Library *Columbus Citizen/Citizen-Journal* Collection (CCJ), the *Columbus Dispatch* (CD), columbusrailroads.com (CRR), *Short North Gazette* (SNG) and the authors' personal collection (PC).

In attempting to set down the history of this great "temple of commerce," we have relied on a variety of sources, not all of which are in agreement when it comes to names, dates, places and events. Where discrepancies occur, we have done our best to either reconcile or note them, but others have undoubtedly crept in when we weren't looking.

Introduction

Columbus is my hometown and I love it. But like the Tin Man, it has no heart. It lost its heart on August 28, 2004, when the iconic Lazarus sign on the department store's High Street façade was dismantled and carted away.

As Jennifer Hambrick of the *Short North Gazette* observed one year later, "The center of Columbus life for more than a century was excised without ceremony. It takes time to bounce back from something like that." It may also take a visit to the Wizard.

Columbus has many things going for it, the types of things that many midwestern cities can only dream about. For one thing, it is growing. For another, it has a diverse economy. It is technologically sophisticated. It is regarded as a good place to live and a good place to do business. And its best days still lie ahead (we hope). However, like many cities, the sidewalks roll up at 5:00 p.m.—at least in the downtown. It wasn't always that way.

"High Street was once like the Easter Parade on 5th Avenue in New York City," author I. David Cohen recalled in *Sorry, Downtown Columbus Is Closed*. "The women wore dresses, gloves and hats. They were dressed to the nines. The men wore fedoras and snappy suits."

Time was when people shopped at Lazarus until midnight or later on Saturdays. More recently, it remained open until 9:30 p.m. on Monday and Thursday evenings, forcing its competitors to do likewise. When Lazarus was open, everything was open.

Cohen argued that the '40s, '50s and '60s made up the golden era in the city's history. In 1950, the residential population of downtown Columbus

On August 28, 2004, the iconic Lazarus sign was quietly taken down and carted away. *JH.*

was 29,845. Fifty years later, the number had dropped to 3,455! During the decade before its closing, sales at the main Lazarus store had declined 60 percent.

Sherry Buk, former executive director of the Columbus Historical Society, remembers changing into her best dress and white gloves before making a Saturday afternoon trip to Columbus to shop. To a young girl from the country, the downtown Lazarus store "was the most elegant thing I'd ever seen in my life." She is far from the only one who felt that way.

While people are slowly moving back to the center city, it is a vastly different place. Gone are the stately old hotels: the Fort Hayes, the Deshler-Wallick and the Neil House. Gone are the landmark restaurants: Benny Klein's, Marzetti's, Mill's Cafeteria, Kuenning's, Seafood Bay and the Maramor. Gone are the first-run movie palaces: the Majestic, the Grand, the Broad, the Palace and the Ohio (although the latter two survive as live performance venues). And gone, too, are the major stores: the Union, the Boston Store, Madison's, Moby's, Morehouse-Fashion and, last but far from least, Lazarus.

Columbus grew up with Lazarus and vice versa. For more than 150 years, the Lazarus family profited from the patronage of Columbus citizenry, and in return, the city benefited from the dollars that flowed through this incredible economic engine. At its height, Lazarus controlled one-third of the retail activity in the city, a feat that no other store in the country ever matched.

The story of the Lazarus is a story of enterprise, perseverance, gumption, innovation, loyalty, commitment, family and change. Lots of change. It is also a story of the love between a store and a community.

"There has been a love affair," Robert Lazarus Jr. told columnist Mike Harden. "The downtown store has a sentimental place in people's hearts. It was, for so many, something special."

The Lazari (as the family called themselves) did not hide from the public. They were listed in the phone book. Bob Jr. says that it was never a problem because people always respected them. When a customer called late one evening, it was to ask the proper way to serve tea (which Robert's father took the time to patiently explain). Unlike many modern-day captains of industry, they didn't feel a need to have bodyguards for their children. But Lazarus is now history. "Inconceivable!" (As Vizzini in *The Princess Bride* would say.)

Inconceivable, indeed. Certainly, such a thought never crossed my mind during the summer I worked for Booker Lucas out of the extra desk at the downtown store. The plastic Lazarus badge pinned to my shirt was my passport to another world. Behind the scenes was an Escherseque array of chutes, tubes, monorails, conveyor belts, stairways, elevators and tunnels, connecting the far-flung corners of the store like secret passages in a gothic novel.

I imagined myself to be one of the brutish Morlocks, toiling underground in service of the beautiful Eloi who worked out on the selling floor (especially Myra and the other young ladies at the cosmetics counters). But unlike the creatures in H.G. Wells's *The Time Machine*, I didn't resent my station in life. I relished it. I felt like a kid at Disneyland exploring this parallel universe, unseen and unsuspected by the thousands of customers who swarmed daily through the store.

Fred Lazarus Jr. said that a department store should be like a big circus, and during much of its run, Lazarus was that and more. "They didn't just sell things," Jan Whittaker, author of *Service and Style: How the American Department Store Fashioned the Middle Class*, wrote of the great family department stores. "They had fashion shows daily, radio shows for kids and charm schools for teenagers"—not to mention an alligator. For eighteen years, Lazarus kept a live alligator in the basement.

When I told people that I was writing a book about Lazarus, the response was always, "I loved that store!" In *Look to Lazarus*, my wife, daughter and I attempt to explain why. We also hope to convey to younger generations what a truly wonderful place these grand emporiums were. Sadly, there is nowhere left they can go to experience what it was like when Lazarus and its kindred institutions were in their heyday.

"Selling is the heart of retail, and satisfying the customer is the heart of that," as Fred Jr. would say, but now that heart has been stilled. Although the memories may have grown fonder over time, the truth is it was a special place, and regrettably, we will not see its like again.

Not all change is progress.

–David Meyers

Note: Unless it is clear from the context, we have adopted the following naming conventions: Simon Lazarus, the founder of the dynasty, will generally be identified as "Simon." Fred and Ralph, his sons (and partners), will usually be designated as "Fred" or "Fred Sr." and "Ralph," respectively. Fred's sons will be referred to as "Uncle Fred" (Fred Jr.), "Uncle Si" (Simon), "Uncle Jack" (Jeffrey) and "Uncle Bob" (Robert).

Chapter 1

Life Before Lazarus

Much of the world forbids slavery, uses the metric system and drives on the right side of the road thanks to Napoleon (Bonaparte, that is, not the other two). While he has been justly credited with these and other accomplishments, much less is made of his contribution to ready-to-wear clothing. Yet the garment industry definitely got a jump-start thanks to the Napoleonic Wars.

In 1800, all clothing was made by tailors, dressmakers and housewives hand-crafting items of attire with a particular wearer in mind. However, this was to change virtually overnight when Napoleon conscripted tens of thousands of soldiers into his army, all of whom were in need of uniforms.

To meet the sudden demand, a few enterprising businessmen obtained contracts to supply uniforms for the emperor's forces and then hired small groups of women to make them. For a dozen or so years, seamstresses worked at home or in small shops for very little money, turning out trousers, blouses, coats and jackets as quickly as their nimble fingers could manage. It was a tedious process and didn't immediately affect the way most people obtained their wearing apparel—especially Napoleon (any of them).

By the 1830s, however, a sea change had taken place. Sailors began patronizing "slop shops" when they were in port. Here they could buy (and sell) used clothing and "slops"—off the-rack items that had often been fabricated in-house. Although they were cheaply made and ill-fitting, "slops" appealed to the seafarers because they were seldom ashore long enough to order a custom-made suit of clothes.[1]

The term dates back to the sixteenth century, when it referred to wide breeches with broad knees that were considered unfit even for pigs, hence "slops" (not that pigs wore pants, of course). The sailors stored their civilian clothing in "slop chests" when they were aboard ship. Since the proprietors of these establishments weren't concerned with repeat business, they made slops from recycled (or "shoddy") cloth and low-grade wool, which quickly unraveled.

Another important market for cheap, ready-made clothing was southern plantation owners who purchased pants and shirts in large quantities to dress out their slaves. Neither fashion nor fit were priorities when it came to clothing field hands—nor prison inmates, for that matter (yet another market for "uniforms," though of a different stripe).

The 1840 U.S. Census showed that there were 57,565 retail stores in the country, representing an average investment of $4,350 each. Competition among dry goods, furniture and specialty stores was particularly cutthroat, owing to the low margin on items. Most people had little disposable income, so they were careful how they spent it. As a result, shop owners endeavored to increase their profits by expanding their lines of merchandise.

In retrospect, it might seem like a small thing, but at the time it was viewed by some as downright evil. Within a decade, one newspaper was railing against a Philadelphia dry goods store for "going beyond its province" by daring to sell umbrellas, parasols and canes. Local ministers, fearing that the "Department Store Octopus" would strangle smaller merchants, denounced it from the pulpit.

Clothing production entered the industrial age with the introduction and refinement of the first practical sewing machines, starting in the 1840s. Then, as the country was plunged into civil war following the attack on Fort Sumter on April 12, 1861, manufacturers began building factories to fulfill the backlog of orders for military uniforms. Hundreds of thousands of men marched off to war, each sporting a new blue or gray uniform.

Arguably, the most important development in the history of ready-made clothing up to this point was the government's publication of detailed measurements of soldiers. For the first time, garments were produced for a range of standardized sizes—for men, anyway—that reoccurred with predictable regularity. It would take another century before a coordinated effort was made to do the same for women's sizes.

By 1848, Rochester, New York, had at least thirty shops at which clothing was made and sold. A decade earlier, German immigrant Myer Greentree had settled in the city and started turning out men's suits for the wholesale trade using standard patterns he had created. Others soon followed, and it wasn't long before there were 1,800 people employed in the city's clothing industry.

A key factor in Rochester's becoming a major clothing center (and America's first "boomtown") was the city's location on the Erie Canal, providing a convenient and economical means for transporting goods westward to Lake Erie. Before the century's end, about six thousand people were at work in Rochester's ready-to-wear industry.

Nearly four hundred miles away in Ohio, things were somewhat different. Columbus was the state capital and little else. The new statehouse building, begun in 1839 and mired in controversy, remained unfinished.[2] Two of the most impressive edifices in town were the Ohio State Penitentiary on the west side and the Ohio Lunatic Asylum on the east, both built with taxpayer dollars. More than four thousand people had fled the city during a cholera outbreak in the summer of 1850. Still, with the population approaching eighteen thousand, there were opportunities aplenty.

Historian Jacob Henry Studer claimed that more improvements were made to the city during the period 1849 to 1853 than during any previous four-year span:

> *Among the large structures erected were the new market house building, on Fourth street, between Town and Rich streets; the Gwynne Block, with its spacious and commodious store rooms, on Town street; numerous large and substantial buildings on High street, and fine residences on Town street, together with structures of various kind throughout the whole city.*

The Central Market House was a hub of social and mercantile activity. For many years, all city offices were housed on the second floor, while three mornings a week, as well as Saturday nights, all manner of goods could be purchased from stalls on the ground floor.[3] Think of it as the city's first shopping mall.

Although Columbus was not directly located on either of the state's major canals, a twelve-mile long feeder canal was opened in 1831, connecting it to the Ohio-Erie Canal ("the Big Ditch") at Lockbourne. This enabled the city to receive large shipments of goods that could not be readily transported by wagon.

When Charles Dickens came to Columbus from Cincinnati by mail coach in 1842, he was pleased to find that he would be traveling along a macadamized (crushed stone) road at the rate of six miles an hour ("rare blessing!"). Most of what were called highways in those days were barely passable, save in the best of weather.

A rough sketch of the Lazarus family's arrival in America, taken from an unpublished history of the store. *EH.*

On February 22, 1850, the Columbus and Xenia Railroad made its maiden run from Columbus to Xenia, a distance of fifty-four miles. Following on its heels was the Cleveland, Columbus and Cincinnati Railroad a year later. Union Depot, a "big, wooden shed," had been built to accommodate the trains and their passengers. By 1872, five locally financed railroads were in operation, propelling the city on its way to becoming a major railroad center.

This was how things stood in 1850 or 1851 when Simon Lazarus arrived in Columbus from the kingdom of Württemberg, accompanied by his wife, Amelia Madeweiss; a stepson from her first marriage, David (who took the Lazarus name); and a son, Fred, born in 1850. Another son, Ralph, would be born in 1852.

Amelia, who probably was a widow when she married Simon, also had a daughter, Fannie. Even though she could not have been much more than thirteen or fourteen, Fannie did not accompany her mother and brother to America. She is believed to have married and had a family of her own.

Although forty-three or forty-four at the time, Simon had been lured to the United States by letters from relatives—the Aronsons (or Aaronsons)—who had preceded him. According to the city directory, there were several Aronsons residing in Columbus: L., P. and R.

In 1892, I.M. Schlesinger, Simon's contemporary, wrote:

> *Judah Nusbaum, a native of Bavaria, Germany, arrived here in the year 1838; Nathan and Joseph Gundersheimer in 1840. All three were traveling*

traders and made their headquarters in Columbus until a few years later,
when they commenced a general store in the Walcutt building, at the corner
of High and Town streets. Simon Mack, S. Lazarus and three brothers,
Samuel, Hess and Abraham Amburg, came here to reside in the year 1844.
In 1847 came Breidenstuhl, of Rochester, S. Schwalbe, S. Morrison and
a half-brother of S. Lazarus named Aaronson.

Schlesinger was clearly mistaken on at least one point: Simon Lazarus did not emigrate from Germany until after the birth of his son, Fred, in May 1850.

In the 1840s, the four Gundersheimer brothers, the two Nusbaums and Sam Amburgh were working as peddlers in and around Columbus. This was an easy occupation in which people of little or no means could get a start. Sometimes other businessmen would "stake" them in exchange for as much as 70 percent of their earnings.

By the middle of the decade, Judah Nusbaum had opened a store, as had Nathan and Joseph Gundersheimer. Within months after his arrival, Simon Lazarus and his half-brother were partners in B. Aronson & Brother, a clothing store located on South High Street between Rich and Mound. Their inventory may have included suits and caps made by R. Aronson, the tailor in the family.

Not long afterward, Sam Amburgh, Simon Mack and Sam Nusbaum also opened stores, and by the end of the decade they were joined by Jacob and Joseph Goodman. In fact, every Jewish family who came to Columbus before 1855 entered the clothing business. All of them were clustered together on South High Street.

As of 1872, German Jewish immigrants owned every clothing store in Columbus, according to historian Marc Lee Raphael. Those listed in *Bailey's Columbus Directory* were Henry Harmon, Joseph Goodman, Jos. Gundersheimer, Louis Kahn, H&N Gundersheimer, Simon Lazarus, Abe Gundersheimer, Arnold Steinhauser, J&H Margolinsky, B&W Frankel, Samuel Amburgh, Samuel Adler & Brother, Judah Nusbaum, Raphael Vogel, Isaac Hoffman, Leo Strauss, Adolph Aaron and Elias Lehman.

Pioneering newspaperman Joel Buttles recorded in his diary that the Germans called people who lived west of the Scioto, many of whom came from Virginia, "Pinchguts" owing to their stinginess, while those who came from New England were "Cold Dumplings."

After the war, the expertise gained through the mass production of military uniforms was applied to the manufacture of ready-to-wear "gent's furnishings." Shop owners looked to middlemen to provide them with the selection they needed for their stores. Simon Lazarus, for one, bet on the fact that soldiers returning to civilian life would be more accepting of ready-made clothing.

In addition to the gains made by technology, the ready-to-wear market was aided by a change in popular fashion. Men began to favor looser-fitting garments that did not require precise tailoring. Tailors recognized that there was money to be made by producing suits for the off-the-rack trade during lulls in their regular business activity. They might sell these out of their own shops or through other merchants.

Most women's clothing, however, continued to be custom-made well into the first decade or two of the twentieth century. From 1878 to 1928, for instance, the wife and daughters of Fred Lazarus had their dresses made by Mary McCormack.[4] The exceptions were such articles as cloaks, corsets and hoop skirts, which could be mass produced since they did not require an exact fit. Hats and shoes were among the last items to benefit from the industrial revolution simply because standardized sizes had not been developed.

None of the early Jewish merchants left behind a written account of these years. However, William G. Dunn, who opened a dry goods business in April 1869, probably spoke for many of them when he wrote:

> *I chose Columbus because it was pleasantly and centrally situated with a good prospect for enlargement; also because the dry goods business there did not seem to be overdone, and was conducted upon the old time plans, trade being held to each store mainly by the influence of the salesman and credits, as it still is in many country stores.*

In his first year, Dunn generated $170,000 in sales, drawing customers not only from Columbus but also from the surrounding communities. Obviously, he and many others found the young city a good place to do business.

Chapter 2

One-Price Store

It's entirely possible that Simon Lazarus and his family stepped off a canalboat moored at the foot of West Broad Street, as one writer asserted a century later. It's also possible that he was wearing a money belt under his coat stuffed with $3,000 in cash. And he may have even spent the better part of a month looking for the right location to open a shop. However, such precise details are more likely the province of a storyteller than a historian.

What is indisputable is that this immigrant from Prussia came to Columbus about 1850 to make a new start. A former rabbinical student, he may have been fleeing religious persecution in his own country. By then, all gains in basic rights made during a series of revolutions that had swept through the German states had been reversed. It was a good time to leave.

We may never know what Simon's occupation was in the old country, how he was able to save $3,000 or why he entered the clothing business. Rabbi Raphael believes that B. Aronson & Brother was actually founded in 1851 by brothers Lazarus Aronson of Columbus and B. Aronson of Philadelphia.[5] (In fact, there was an L. Aronson listed in the city directory, but no B.) Rather than starting from scratch, Simon probably invested in his half-brother's existing men's store and, not long afterward, became the sole owner.

The shop was twenty feet wide by thirty or forty feet deep (or fourteen by seventy, depending on the source). It may have originally been located between Rich and Mound, but by 1858 it was in the center of the Parsons Building, between Town and Rich Streets. He soon rented an adjoining space as well, enlarging the store at 153 (formerly 163) South High Street to one hundred feet deep.

Simon and Amelia
Lazarus came to
America in search of
religious freedom and
found much more. *PC.*

A listing for the store would not appear in the Columbus city directory until 1856–57, by which time the enigmatic "B. Aronson" was definitely living in Philadelphia. The establishment's clientele was largely drawn from the ranks of city and state government officials, all of whom were male. Its proximity to the well-known United States Hotel and the well-traveled National Road was said to be important to its early success.

Although there were more than a few clothing merchants in Columbus in 1851, only one advertised regularly in the local papers: the United States Clothing Store at the corner of South High and State Streets. Operated by E. and M.S. Hess, it claimed to have the largest assortment of ready-made clothing in the city, including coats, frocks, overcoats, wrappers, pantaloons, vests, shirts, handkerchiefs, undershirts, drawers, suspenders, shirt collars, traveling trunks, carpet bags and so on, all at least 30 percent cheaper than anywhere else "this side of the Eastern cities."

As early as 1849, the Gundersheimers, Nusbaums and others had begun holding Friday night services under the title H'nai Jeshuren, as required by Jewish law. According to I.M. Schlesinger, Simon Lazarus served as their rabbi (although he had yet to arrive in Columbus) without remuneration, and Nathan Gundersheimer was president of the congregation. The families met upstairs in a building later known as the Twin Brothers Clothing Store.

When Simon became a clothing merchant, it was a relatively new field. Male tailors made apparel for men and boys that they either sold themselves or through vendors of "gent's furnishings." Female dressmakers and milliners fashioned clothing for women and girls. The supplies required to create the items (i.e., fabric, fancy goods and notions) were purchased from a dry goods store. More than fifty tailors and dressmakers plied their trade in Columbus.

Coincidentally, in September 1851, Isaac M. Singer announced in newspapers across the country that his "Patent, Straight Needle, Perpendicular Action Sewing Machine" could be purchased for $125 from his offices in New York, Boston or Philadelphia. Singer claimed that the machine would "perform the labor of from five to ten persons, depending on the kind of work and skill of the operator."

Within a year, William Burdell, a Columbus merchant, advertised the "new way" of making clothing by comparing it to such technological marvels as the railroad and the telegraph. His message was clear: the manufacture of clothing had entered a new era, the industrial age.

Also in September 1851, Graham's New York One-Price Store opened for business at 172 South High Street between Friend and Rich Streets. Possibly inspired by Graham's example, Simon adopted the one-price policy, too. Historically, merchants did not price their merchandise but rather expected customers to haggle with them. Given Simon's unfamiliarity with the English language (he was said to be cordial but quiet), posting prices on items would have greatly simplified transactions.

At the beginning of the decade, Columbus proper was bounded by Naghten Street (originally North Public Lane) on the north, Livingston Avenue on the south, Washington Street on the east and the Scioto River on the west. Simon's store, a couple of blocks south of the partially constructed state capitol building, was in easy walking distance from anywhere, although the streets were unpaved and the sidewalks no more than rough wooden planks.

During the 1850s, much of the country was seized by "western fever." Consequently, the steady increase in population was offset by the continual westward migration. Nevertheless, population growth in Columbus resumed during the next decade, even as many young men were dying in the Civil War. In 1850, it had been 17,882. Ten years later, it numbered 18,554. By 1870, it was 31,274.

Despite getting a later start than the Gundersheimers and the Nusbaums, Simon quickly made up for lost time. In 1864, he purchased an adjoining shoe store for $2,100, allowing him to expand his frontage on South High. By 1876, when he bought an adjacent vacant lot for $7,800, he was ranked as "one of the substantial businessmen of Columbus." He also won two awards at the Ohio State Fair, one for the best hand-made "suit of gent's clothing" and the other for the best machine-made.

Nathan Gundersheimer was operating his business out of his home, but Simon rented separate living quarters for his family not far from his shop. As children, his sons Fred and Ralph (and, no doubt, stepson David) worked in the store before school, carrying water from the Scioto River to mop the floor each morning. Sometimes they would have to break holes in the ice. After school, they returned to the store to help out in other ways. Fred also sold the morning paper, picking up copies at 4:30 a.m. so that he could get out on the streets to hawk them before dawn.

Like most of his competitors, Simon did little if any advertising until after the Civil War, relying strictly on word of mouth. However, F.D. Clark of the New York Clothing Store at 121 South High Street was an exception. His ads in the local newspapers even mentioned his "cutter" (tailor), J.H. Parsons.

Another frequent advertiser was Marcus Childs, who operated out of the Neil House building at 6 and 7 South High Street. In 1863, Childs offered ready-made clothing for men, boys and "military gentlemen." He also had a "merchant tailoring department." On December 11, 1865, Childs commenced a going-out-of-business sale, having decided to retire. At the same time, Stebbins, Towne & Company was holding a closeout sale of all clothing, hats, caps and gentlemen's furnishing goods.

Although Ohio contributed men, money and management to the Civil War, no major battles were fought here. But in the spring of 1863, Confederate general John Hunt Morgan and some 2,500 of his cavalry rode deep into the southern region of the state. His intent was to join the army of General Robert E. Lee in Pennsylvania. Instead, the raiders were cornered in Columbiana County on July 26 and forced to surrender.

While Morgan and a handful of his officers were locked up in the Ohio Penitentiary, the rest of his troops were confined at Camp Chase military prison beyond the western boundary of the city on Sullivant Avenue. At both places, the prisoners of war were accorded better treatment than their fellow inmates. In fact, the commander of Camp Chase, Reverend Granville Moody, allowed them to sign themselves out on their "parole" (word) so they could freely roam the city during the day.

According to Lazarus family lore, a few of Morgan's Raiders once entered the store and stole some clothing.[6] When the theft was discovered, Fred and Ralph grabbed some guns and made a surprise visit to Camp Chase. They purportedly found the rebel soldiers in their quarters with the stolen merchandise and "got the goods back." The Lazarus boys wouldn't have been more than twelve to fourteen years old. Perhaps they were accompanied by stepbrother David, who was six years older than Fred.

Charles Lazarus described his great-grandfather, Simon, as a "very aggressive, but quiet man." When the soldiers returned from the war in 1865, he realized that he needed to be prepared for them. Therefore, he drove a horse and buggy to Rochester, New York, and returned with two hundred ready-made suits. "He was always planning for the future."

"They were buying clothes and doing away with their army blue and the clothing business was good," Fred Lazarus Sr. recalled in 1908. "The soldiers had money and were willing to spend it. Soldiers would go into the basement of the new store and change their army togs for the store clothes."

One veteran who had exchanged his uniform for a new set of clothes left $400 in the pocket. A month later, he came back in search of it. "Mr. Lazarus remembered that when the man had changed clothes he threw his uniform trousers into the air, glad to be free of them." They found the pants had gotten snagged on a nail in the basement ceiling and still contained his bankroll.[7]

Simon's gamble paid off. In the 1866 Columbus city directory, "S. Lazarus" was described as a "dealer in ready-made clothing." He purportedly had abandoned the B. Aronson & Brother name about a decade earlier.

Within two years, the business had grown to the point where it employed seven salesmen in addition to Simon's two young sons. The Lazarus family attributes their patriarch's success to his boldness and his cultivation of a reputation for honesty and quality. Meanwhile, David Lazarus, Simon's twenty-five-year-old stepson, had married and moved north to Warren, Ohio, where he also became a clothing merchant.

In 1870, Lazarus became the first store in Ohio to make home deliveries by wagon, albeit only one per day. Simon quickly discontinued this service, however, after his only horse was involved in a collision with a streetcar. It wasn't until after his death that wagon deliveries were resumed.

Columbus was soon home to some two hundred menswear stores, most destined to fail by the turn of the century. There were seven sewing machine agents who supplied the forty dressmakers and twenty-seven tailors, as well as the numerous cloak makers, eighteen milliners and one maker of hoop skirts. The industry employed more than 750 workers, with aggregate sales of nearly $8.7 million. One manufacturing house alone, English, Miller & Company, had more than 150 workers. Remarkably, two of the tailors were women—Kate Lawrence and Mrs. Ingham. Somehow they had broken into an almost exclusively male arena, although the demand for their services was quickly diminishing.

Chapter 3
A Fit or No Sale

Unlike their father, Fred and Ralph grew up in the United States and knew the country's customs and language from childhood. They had also been around the store nearly all their lives. While Simon had made at least one or two false starts in his choice of careers, his sons were groomed to be merchants. They may have been reared in a German-speaking household, but they lived in a predominantly English-speaking town. Columbus was all they knew.

In 1874, S. Lazarus, clothier, officially became S. Lazarus & Sons. This was in recognition of the fact that Fred Lazarus, age twenty-two, and Ralph Lazarus, twenty, had joined their father as full partners in the business, "sharing his firm views on customer service and fairness." It also was an acknowledgement that Simon was getting old (he was sixty-seven) and that his health was becoming a concern. Succession planning had begun.

As of 1875, the following retail clothing dealers were located in downtown Columbus, nearly all of them within a few blocks of one another:

- Aaron, 7 South High Street.
- S. Amburg, 127 South High Street.
- J. Goodman, 1 South High Street.
- H&N Gundersheimer, 101 South High Street.
- Gundersheimer, 205 South High Street.
- Jos. Gundersheimer, 81 and 83 South High Street.
- R. Gundersheimer, 213 South High Street.
- A.N. Hill & Company, 45 South High Street.

A Fit or No Sale

After becoming F&R Lazarus & Company in 1877, the store quickly began to expand into the adjacent properties. *PC.*

- L. Kahn, 97 South High Street.
- S. Lazarus, 139 South High Street.
- E. Lehman, 172 East Friend Street (i.e., Main Street).
- I&H Margolinksy, 204 South High Street.
- A. Steinhauser, 183 South High Street.
- R. Vogel, 359 South High Street.

Two years later, seventy-year-old Simon Lazarus was dead. His grandson, Robert Lazarus Sr., later described him as "a good man, a gentle man, a scholar—and no merchant." Perhaps. But even more important than the store that bore his name was the name itself, built on a carefully nurtured reputation for honesty. That was his enduring legacy to his children.

Upon their father's death, Fred and Ralph, joined by their mother, Amelia, set about expanding the store. They started by purchasing the Fassig Shoe Store directly north of them for $3,500, increasing the space for their clothing line to 3,200 square feet. They also opened a branch store at 6 North High Street, later the site of the Deshler Hotel.

The manager of the new venture was Abraham B. Cohen, Simon's son-in-law, who had married Rosalie Lazarus. Ads in local newspapers informed customers, "We employ a small army of tailors, have two first

29

In 1872, Abe Cohen was given his own merchant tailor store because Fred and Ralph Lazarus didn't like working with him. *PC.*

class cutters, carry a large line of piece goods. Our guarantee stands good, 'A Fit or No Sale.'" It was the same promise Simon had made to returning Civil War veterans.

Charles Lazarus later claimed that they opened the first branch store simply because Cohen was "impossible to work with." What made matters worse, Abe and his bride were living with Fred, Ralph and their widowed mother. The branch store, later bearing the address 13 North High Street, continued to operate for seventeen years or so, finally closing in about 1894.[8]

The Lazarus brothers, who were unusually close, divided up their duties, with Ralph taking responsibility for creating all advertising copy and Fred attending to the business side of the enterprise. Amelia's self-appointed responsibility was to go to the store each day and count the money. According to family historian Charlotte Witkind (Amelia's great-granddaughter), "She didn't trust her kids to be entirely responsible." Certainly they were not as frugal as their father.

In the company's history, Amelia was the only female member of the family to occupy a position of prominence. Lazarus women simply weren't considered for roles in the business, although they were encouraged to involve themselves in civic and charitable affairs. When women eventually did rise through the ranks—and there would be many—they were not Lazarus women.

Elder son Fred had a penchant for strolling through the store each day, striking up conversations with employees and customers alike. More often than not, he would buy a gift for any small child he might encounter. Witkind claimed that if her grandfather saw that the man selling papers outside the store needed a new pair of shoes, he would invite him in to get a pair for free.

Fred was also generous when it came to local charities. He was the first person to make a contribution when the Knights of Columbus kicked off a building campaign, despite its being a Roman Catholic organization. He simply liked all people, regardless of race, religion or ethnicity, and didn't hesitate to share his good fortune with others.

Ralph, too, was fairly liberal with his money. Once, while his brother was in Germany "taking the cure" at a health spa (which they did a few times a year), Ralph teamed up with five partners to buy the Southern Hotel. His share of the deal was $250,000, which he withdrew from their joint bank account without even bothering to consult Fred. He didn't need to.

The policy of giving a free cigar with every suit purchase probably began with Ralph. "If we said, 'Step back to my office, son, and get Mr. Smith one of our fine Three Brothers cigars,' it meant that the man had just bought a $10 suit," Robert Lazarus (Fred's son) recalled. "They were called Three Brothers, I think, because if one brother smoked the cigar, the other two had to carry him out. We had proportionately better cigars to the $20 and $30 and $40 suit customers."

From a personality standpoint, Fred and Ralph could not have been more different. For relaxation, Fred liked to fish; Ralph preferred to take long walks. While Fred married and raised a family, Ralph had little interest in women. In fact, he was adamantly against having them work in the store in any capacity, even at secretarial positions. While a lot can be read into this, he apparently did not object to female shoppers as long as they did not cross paths with the male customers.

A stylish dresser, Ralph contributed to the store's success through his approach to buying and advertising. He was known to knock off ad copy in three minutes' time while standing in the newspaper office. When he died, the lifelong bachelor left no heirs, so control of the store was passed down through his brother's line.

Fred, by contrast, had five sons, one of whom died in infancy. The remaining four—Simon ("Uncle Si"), Fred Jr. ("Uncle Fred"), Robert

("Uncle Bob") and Jeffrey ("Uncle Jack")—all played a part in the store's subsequent development. When Fred decreed that everyone who worked for the store was an associate, not an employee, his sons ensured that this policy continued even after his death.

One hot Fourth of July, Fred noticed that a nearby bank had closed promptly at 3:00 p.m., leaving a long line of Civil War veterans waiting to cash their pension checks. He immediately decided to institute a free check-cashing service. He was not only honoring the veterans for their service, but he also suspected that more than a few of them would turn around and spend some of the money in his store. He was right.

By all accounts, Fred was loved and respected by everyone. During an interview with the Jewish Historical Society, Charles recalled that his grandfather "had a wonderful way of dealing with the grandchildren. He'd put us over his knee and slap us on the behind and pennies would fall out on the floor."

The importance of such strong personalities in the leadership of the Lazarus store should not be underestimated. Even as it grew from its humble beginnings to a multimillion-dollar enterprise, it was still perceived as a family business, concerned for and responsive to the local community. By the time it reached the billion-dollar mark, however, the family was no longer in charge, and the warm and fuzzy feelings were rapidly dissipating.

Chapter 4

Square Dealing Clothiers

With Simon's passing in 1877, the store changed names once again, this time to F&R Lazarus & Company. It probably should have been FR&A. While Fred and Ralph may have handled all of the buying, bookkeeping, copywriting and a good measure of the selling, they continued to receive considerable assistance from their mother, Amelia.

Free to chart their own course, the brothers quickly moved to modernize the store. They also introduced giveaway programs, such as free shoe shines with every pair of shoes, and continued to purchase more of the neighboring real estate. Although their father's photo continued to hang in the store, they had quickly emerged from his shadow.

The store's first annual financial statement in 1880 gave sales as $64,732. Within a year, Lazarus employed twenty-two clerks, and sales had jumped to $81,329. Early the same decade, Lazarus expanded further into two additional storerooms, including Harvey Coit's Clothing House to the south, and in 1891 added George R. Elliott's third-floor photography studio. By then, it had become the biggest clothing dealer in central Ohio, known for quality merchandise at low prices—"square dealing clothiers."

From 1872 to 1887, the store's address changed from 139 South High Street to 135–141 South High Street as they acquired more real estate. Then, in 1888, it became 167–171 South High Street, due to a change in the way the city lots were numbered. The "Lazarus Block" occupied High Street between Town and Walnut.

A typical ad from 1885 read:

To the Public in General. We Sound a Warning—Be Careful Of Sham Clothing Sales and wonderful Aladdin Tales of "Must be Sold Overstock," and for thirty or sixty day Sales. We can't give our goods away; but buy in great quantities, strictly for Cash, as we will sell with a small profit. So beware of Shams and Buncombe Sales and trade only at Lazarus' Mammoth Clothing Establishments!

Sometime in the 1880s, sales clerks at the Lazarus and Gundersheimer stores petitioned their employers for shorter hours. They proposed working no later than 8:00 p.m. when busy, 6:00 p.m. when not. During spring and summer, they had often been required to stay as late as 10:00 p.m. to wait on shoppers. It is probably not a coincidence that the first organized employee activity also took place during this period: an outing to the Ohio State Fair.

In 1887, Lazarus opened a family shoe department for men, women and children. It was no longer just a men's store; it was beginning to cast a wider net. Newspapers ads during 1880s featured dapper-looking engravings of Fred and Ralph, initially full-length and later just their heads, reminiscent of the cough drop–touting Smith brothers.

During the 1890s, Ralph and Fred Lazarus were portrayed in ads for the main store and its branch. *PC.*

A common belief among retailers was that male customers were reluctant to patronize a store that offered women's clothing. Therefore, Lazarus ensured that gent's furnishings were placed close to the main door so men could come in, get what they wanted and leave without encountering any female shoppers.

Department store historian Jan Whittaker wrote that men were "loyal to the store, less prone to comparison shop than women, and less likely than women to handle the merchandise." In other words, they were exactly the kind of customers every store wanted. Women, on the other hand, could be problematic.

Nevertheless, Fred and Ralph made the conscious decision that their store would cater to everyone—men, women, children and minorities. At a time when many stores openly discriminated against African Americans, Lazarus welcomed them—and their money.

Macy's in New York and Wanamaker's in Philadelphia were already full-fledged "department stores," but Lazarus was still evolving. As wooden archways lighted with gas lamps were being erected over High Street in 1888 to mark the 100th anniversary of the Northwest Territory, the store advertised it had seven electric lights and all modern improvements.[9] According to an unpublished history of the store, Columbus had become the wealthiest city per capita in the country.

At the beginning of the next decade, Columbus had a dress factory and dress-cutting school operated by Mr. and Mrs. Higgs. She was the only female tailor listed in the city directory at the time. While most women still wore custom-made apparel, a quiet revolution was taking place. The dress-cutting school would be gone within a few years.

Outside a restaurant, Lazarus became the first store in Columbus to offer food when the brothers installed the Niagara Soda Fountain in 1891. Constructed of white travertine marble, it cost $1,600 and had twenty-five stools. With eight flavors of floats, sarsaparillas and other confections, it was an immediate success. Years later, Doral Chenoweth, the "Grumpy Gourmet," wrote, "If the customer wanted it gassed, that meant a mixture of birch oil and sassafras spiked with carbonation." (See Appendix II.)

The year 1895 saw the construction of the Lazarus Electric Light Department across Town Street. Connected to the store by a tunnel running under the pavement, it supplied power to the eight hundred electric light bulbs that outlined the newly erected Renaissance clock tower. The arch over High Street was electrified as well. Overnight, the store was transformed into the most dazzling landmark in the city.

Three times a day, the power plant's steam whistle blasted weather signals. Free whistle code cards were distributed so patrons could interpret them. Floorwalker Fred King, "the handsomest man in the store," was assigned to go out in the street when the whistle blew to calm the horses tied up at the hitching posts. "It was very loud and could cause runaways," he explained.

Electric lights were a new phenomenon when Lazarus used them to outline its Mammoth Store. *CML.*

Beginning in 1895, Lazarus operated its own power plant to meet its enormous demand for electricity. *David Bunge Collection / CRR.*

One by one, adjoining storefronts had been purchased until the "Lazarus Mammoth Store" spread over half a block and totaled 100,000 square feet on one floor. An orange painted façade at ground level tied the disparate properties together visually, prompting the comment that "the store was held together with paint."

After only nine years in the business, Lazarus had become the largest shoe store in the state. Ladies' shoes sold for two dollars a pair and men's for three dollars. Although many women bought their shoes there, they still had to go elsewhere to purchase dresses and other items of feminine apparel. It would be a few more years before women began to accept ready-to-wear fashions as a replacement for the custom work of dressmakers. However, by 1900, the number of dressmakers had dwindled to 125 (while ladies' tailors increased to 7).

When the Spanish-American War veterans returned home in 1898, 150 Lazarus associates, all men, marched in a parade to welcome them. The same year, Enoch J. Salt, advertising manager for F&R Lazarus, published

The rambling "Lazarus Block" at the southwest corner of Town and High Streets. as it appeared in about 1900. *PC.*

a book entitled *Helps Over Rough Places* in imitation leather paper for a one dollar a copy. It consisted of "a large number of bright, snappy head-lines, interesting phrases and arguments for the use of retailers."

Originally a wholesale grocer from Portsmouth, Salt had moved to Columbus in 1895 to work for Lazarus after serving as president of the Portsmouth City Council. His ads were known for being "truthful and timely." A typical example was: "The bugle call has been sounded and the gathered hosts of newest and prettiest styles in spring footwear await your coming. Here are a few 'flowers of the army' of splendid bargains we offer."

In 1902, the same year the Lazarus bowling league was organized, twenty-year-old Simon, the eldest of the brothers, entered the family business because his Uncle Ralph's health was declining. When Ralph died of cancer a year later at the age of fifty-one, nineteen-year-old Fred Jr., the second oldest, took over his vacated finance position. Four years earlier in 1899, their grandmother, Amelia, had passed away, too, and now Fred Sr.'s health was also raising concerns, although he would live for many more years.

FREE TO OUR BOY FRIENDS

We give each boy his choice of a ball and bat, catcher's glove, mask or fielder's mitt with his suit. They are the best values in Columbus, and not a cent is added on account of the gift. The prices are

2.50, 3.00, 3.50, 4.00, 5.00, 6.50, 8.00, 10.00

Dark shades for Confirmation use

Lazarus

In 1903, a boy would receive a free ball and bat, catcher's glove or fielder's mitt with the purchase of a suit. *PC.*

When the time came to pass the baton to the next generation, Fred Jr. was ready. His father and uncle had prepared him well. At the age of ten, he had started working as a collar salesman every Saturday for twenty-five cents. When he turned eighteen, he began selling shoes. He knew about money. More than any of his predecessors, he established Lazarus on the national stage (while unwittingly setting in motion the events that would ultimately lead to the store's demise).

In 1904, Fred Jr. was able to persuade his father to change the bookkeeping method. Historically, sales had been recorded when the customer paid. However, he argued they should post the sale when the purchase was made as "accounts receivable." This enabled them to keep more accurate inventory records. It wasn't long before this bookkeeping system was adopted by other merchants as well.

The same year, Lazarus staged its first anniversary sale, a two-day event. In later years, it was expanded to a month-long extravaganza, usually in March so that it would precede Easter. Due to the Second World War and the difficulty of procuring goods, the anniversary sale was discontinued in 1942 but returned in 1951 as a five-day celebration.

Two years after Ralph's passing, Jessie Ross, the first female employee, joined Lazarus when the store's two-telephone service (believed to be the first in the country) was expanded to eight. She was not only the company's switchboard operator but also its executive secretary. In effect, she was the corporation's first female officer.

Always quotable, Fred Lazarus Jr. became the public face of the store while still in his twenties. *PC.*

In 1908, French hotel magnate César Ritz is said to have declared (in French, of course), "The customer is never wrong!" A year later, either Harry Gordon Selfridge Jr. or, possibly, his Chicago employer, Marshall Field, gave it a positive spin, asserting, "The customer is always right!"[10]

The Lazarus family had long taken this maxim to heart, and it is frequently cited as one of the reasons why their store was so beloved. If a customer was ever unhappy with anything purchased at Lazarus, she (sometimes he) could always take it back, no questions asked. In practice, the store sometimes accepted returned merchandise that it hadn't even sold just to keep the customer satisfied.

Nearly seventy years later, Fred Jr. recalled that the seven buildings that composed the store were "put together by wall openings and administered through mirrors set at angles so that all sections of the store were visible from an office, which was elevated three steps, and situated about 100 feet back from High Street."

At the time, Fred and Ralph weren't so much concerned with shoplifting as ensuring that every customer received good service so that "the Lazarus name was recognized for its honesty." As Enoch Salt wrote in a 1906 ad, "It would be suicidal to our interests to sell you poor clothes—we know the havoc a dissatisfied patron can create." Other local merchants followed their lead.

The Lazarus store general office from about 1900. *PC.*

An advertising postcard from 1908 promoting the sale of vacation wear. *CML.*

Late in the nineteenth century, Charles I. Hood had risen from stock boy to grocery store owner, a Horatio Alger feat that was all the more remarkable because he was black. His store at 178 South High Street was located across the street from that of his good friends, Fred and Ralph Lazarus. Despite being an African American, Charles told his son, Earl, that the Lazarus family always treated him as an equal. Not surprisingly, he endeavored to model his business after theirs.

According to Earl Hood, his father's take on the Lazarus philosophy was "always give good measure." He credits his father's business, as well as that of his own Earl Hood Orchestra, to the fact that neither of them ever lost sight of their customers' expectations, a trait they shared with the Lazarus family. However, unlike the Lazarus store, Hood's grocery did not survive the bank panic that was ignited in October 1907.

Chapter 5

Ready-to-Wear

Charles Lazarus always said, "The chanciest [decision] the family ever made" was in 1907 when they broke ground on a new six-story, 115,000-square-feet building, despite being in the middle of a nationwide financial crisis. Fred Jr. and young Simon had pushed for the project and eventually persuaded their father to go along.

No one would have blamed their father if he had decided to rest on his laurels. After all, the "Lazarus Mammoth Store" had grown to occupy the first floor of seven adjacent buildings at the southwest corner of Town and High Streets. Annual sales in men's and boy's wear was about $695,000 (the equivalent of about $16 million in 2011). Lazarus dominated the market, and the family lived quite comfortably. The "smart" thing to do would have been to play it safe.

However, Fred Sr. believed that his sons should be encouraged to take greater responsibility for store operations. They had grown up in the business, and they firmly believed that a new wave of ready-to-wear clothing was about to arrive: women's and girl's apparel and accessories. Perhaps he thought back to the gamble his own father had taken when he traveled to Rochester at the end of the Civil War. He gave the plan his full support.

The family purchased the site of the former United States Hotel, just across Town Street from their sprawling store with its landmark clock tower. "We made a loan to build the store, $350,000, and pledged all the family's real estate," Fred Jr. later said. "It was a big risk for the family."

Located at 141 South High Street on the northwest corner of Town and High Streets, it was the only major store built in the United States during

The family's "chanciest" decision paid off when it opened a new store in 1909 at the northwest corner of Town and High Streets. *Donald A. Kaiser Collection/CRR.*

this period. In fact, an estimated 40 percent of medium- and large-sized department stores failed during the years 1905–15.

Simon and Fred Jr. had been right. The economic slump that had enabled them to build a new store relatively cheaply benefited them in other ways as well. Because ready-made clothing was less expensive than dressmaker apparel, women began to warm up to the idea on the basis of cost alone. However, a fashion rebellion was also taking place.

The dressy fashions of the time were closely fitted. In order to get over this hurdle, ladies' ready-to-wear clothing consisted of separates (i.e., a shirtwaist with a separate skirt) and one-size-fits-all items (e.g., the flounced wrapper and the Dolman cloak). All of these items could be mass-produced on sewing assembly lines.

The Gibson Girl look of the 1890s had introduced the shirtwaist.[11] With a separate gored skirt and, often, a separate jacket, it became the "uniform" for the first women to work in offices and stores. Up until the passage of the Nineteenth

Amendment in 1920, thousands of suffragettes paraded in shirtwaist outfits. The wrapper had a flounce (a strip of decorative material) around the bottom or at the bosom level, prompting the line, "She flounced out of the room."

Although the economy continued to limp along into the summer of 1908, the year as a whole turned out to be a good one for menswear. The city's retailers attributed the surge in early holiday buying to a series of cartoons in the *Ohio State Journal*. For twenty-one days, artist Harry Westerman found a different way to remind "Bill Putitoff" how many shopping days remained until Christmas. Entering the New Year, expectations continued to be high.

With the new store completed, Lazarus had only to occupy it. Just after 11:00 p.m. on Saturday night, August 14, 1909, as the last customer departed, preparations began. "At 12 o'clock," the local newspaper reported, "the city

In 1908, "Bill Putitoff" reminded the citizens of Columbus how many shopping days were left until Christmas. *PC.*

44

closed off Town Street, and a wooden platform was laid down from curb to curb six feet wide. This was covered with a canopy in case of rain, and everything was put in trucks and moved across to the new building."

Throughout the night, goods were carted from one building to the other, unpacked and arranged for display. Merchandise for new departments was already waiting, as were various fixtures. As a result, the new and improved store was able to open promptly on Monday morning, August 16, with the slogan, "Everything Ready-to-Wear," emblazoned on the electric sign high atop the building.

An ad appeared in Monday's newspapers:

A live chick will break its shell—a dead one never. We have "broken our shell" and have earned the reputation of a "live" concern. We welcome

In 1909, Lady Lazarus welcomed one and all to the new store, the "greatest ready-to-wear concern in the middle west." *PC.*

The Ladies Hosiery, Knit Underwear and Toilet Goods Departments on the main floor. *CML.*

you, one and all, residents of Columbus and the surrounding countryside, to our new home, the largest ready-to-wear concern in the middle west.

While the new building was 101 by 187½ feet and six stories tall, only the first three floors were initially used for selling. Still, it was the largest such establishment in the region, with twenty new departments devoted to women's and girls' apparel and accessories such as cloaks, suits, skirts, petticoats, furs, lingerie, muslin and knit underwear, gloves, corsets, perfumery and belts.

What was originally called the Costume Room or Gown Shop (later the French Room and finally the Wedgewood Room) was created to provide a selection of the highest-quality women's clothing. As expected, the store also offered men's and boy's wear. However, little attention was paid to children's departments, except for infants' wear and shoes.

The ever popular Niagara Soda Fountain was relocated from the old store to the first floor of the new one. There was also an aviary filled with singing canaries. A Customer Lounge, furnished with wicker chairs, Turkish rugs and ferns, occupied the balcony above the first floor. In 1926, it was moved to the fifth floor overlooking Front Street and the Scioto River and renamed the Meeting Place.

A three-story brick stable had been built two years earlier at 34 West Town Street to accommodate seventeen delivery wagons and twenty horses. A bridge

The original women's dress shop on the third floor was called the Costume Room. *CML.*

The Men's Smoking Room on the balcony clearly was intended to encourage the practice. *CML.*

A three-story brick stable was built in 1907 but was later adapted for many other purposes as well. *PC.*

over Wall Street now connected it to the main store. Before it was demolished in 1924, the building had also housed a garage, a Toyland expansion, various special events and the Associates' Cafeteria. The cafeteria provided store employees with good, wholesome meals at the lowest possible cost.

On August 19, 1909, Lazarus unveiled its first escalator, running from the first to the second floor. It proved to be a rickety affair and was removed in 1914 because people were afraid to use it. One patron memorialized the contraption with this bit of doggerel:

> *What's the crowd a pushin' and a shovin' over there?*
> *Land! It's folks a ridin' up the escalator stair!*
> *Ma's brought all the family in to take a little ride,*
> *Cause they're simply goin' dippy*
> *Bout that Escalator Glide![12]*

"People thought we were nuts," Uncle Bob recalled, when they originally announced that they were going to build a new store, but the family was quickly vindicated. Sales for the first year of operations in the new store

Cartoonist Billy Ireland (a Ross County boy himself) drew attention to the store's new moving stairway in 1909. *PC.*

totaled $929,425, nearly doubling the previous year's take (which had been down somewhat due to the panic).

In deference to the sensibilities of its male customers, men's furnishings were placed by the High Street door, and men's clothing was located immediately above with access via a "stag" (men only) elevator. Eight years later in 1917, when the basement was opened for business, the men's department was moved directly below the upstairs department. It could be reached not only by the elevator but also by a stairwell adjacent to the High Street door. Even after the store expanded in 1921, men's clothing continued to occupy the first floor.

The tearoom craze reached Columbus in 1910 when F&R Lazarus opened one to provide a safe haven for ladies to meet in the afternoon. The same year, the company began providing its associates with one week of paid vacation annually. To put this into perspective, Professor Stanley K. Schultz wrote that as recently as the early 1950s, most Americans did not receive a yearly employer-paid vacation.

One person who opened an account in the new store was Mame Thurber, mother of author James Thurber. A rather eccentric character, she would take young Jamie to the store so that they could pretend to be shoplifters.

According to Tom Thomson of the *Short North Gazette*, the floorwalkers soon caught on that it was all a harmless prank. But perhaps she simply misunderstood when the store advertised merchandise for "Next to that which is next to nothing in price."

Three years after the new store debuted, Kinderland was unveiled on the fourth floor. Until then, all sales activity had been restricted to the first three levels. This entirely new department had separate shops for babies, boys' and girls' clothing, children's furnishings, misses' millinery, sporting goods, gifts and even a cottage-sized German Doll Shop. The same year, the first Lazarus delivery trucks took to the streets—no more horse-drawn wagons.

In 1912, Robert Lazarus, twenty-two, joined his father and brothers Fred Jr. and Simon in the family business. During the same year, retail sales exceeded $1 million for the first time. The store established the Lazarus Savings Association, a sort of credit union, for its employees. A savings account could be opened by depositing as little as a quarter.

The following year, store hours were shortened to be from 8:30 a.m. to 6:00 p.m., including Saturdays. The first issue of the *Enthusiast*, a monthly in-house newspaper, rolled off the press in February. A month later on March 25, the "Great Flood of 1913" struck Columbus, engulfing an area from the Scioto River to the Hilltop with up to twenty-two feet of water. Dayton, Ohio, was particularly hard hit.

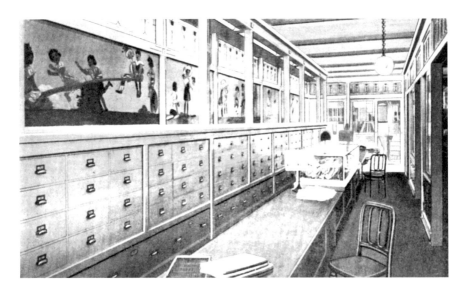

"Kinder" is German for "children," so the Lazarus Kinderland naturally included a Baby Shop. *CML.*

Misses Millinery was another shop in the fourth-floor Kinderland. *CML.*

In 1913, Kinderland opened on the fourth floor, which included a Furnishing Department. *CML.*

Simon was quick to head up the Relief Committee, loaning the store's entire stock of canoes to the effort. Five associates braved the raging waters to rescue stranded west-side residents. When the floodwaters finally receded, ninety-three people were dead, four bridges had been swept away and nearly $6 million

The German Doll Shop occupied this cottage within Kinderland. *CML.*

worth of property had been damaged. Later, Simon and his father, Fred Sr., campaigned for the construction of the levee along the downtown riverfront.

Gradually, the store expanded to occupy the remaining floors of the new building. In 1914, tearooms were installed on the first-floor balcony and the fifth floor (the latter necessarily doubled in size within a year). Other new departments included art needlework, gifts, toys, millinery, yard goods, notions, trimmings, linens and domestics. It seemed as though Lazarus could do no wrong. (See Appendix IV.)

"If you haven't sensed the spirit that permeates the air at Lazarus, then you can't have been here very long," an employee wrote in the *Enthusiast*. "It's here just as surely as the walls and counters." To recognize employee loyalty, Lazarus established the Twenty Year Club with a meeting and banquet. Thirteen charter members were initiated, all male, ranging from twenty-two to fifty years of service.

In 1915, the sixty-fourth anniversary of the Lazarus store was marked by a six-day sale. Some thirty-three thousand customers swarmed the sales floors during the first two days to buy up two hundred lots of discounted merchandise.

"By investing heavily in buying trips to Europe and high fashion," Jonathan Schwartz later wrote, "Lazarus established itself as the arbiter of taste and style in the minds of Columbus shoppers. 'Lazarus customers are not provincials who know nothing outside their own city…[and] Lazarus merchandise represents the best markets in the world.'"

Uncle Fred specialized in finances, Uncle Si in personnel and community relations and Uncle Bob in merchandising and publicity. This "band of brothers" may not have been soldiers entering battle, but they were combatants in the field of commerce. And they did not let many opportunities slip by them. When a driverless electric car smashed through a Lazarus plate-glass window the following year, a sign was swiftly installed proclaiming, "Everything new comes to Lazarus first."

Upon joining the store in 1916, Jeffrey (Uncle Jack) was the youngest at twenty-two. He would have difficulty, however, finding his place in this management troika, in part due to the usual sibling rivalry. This situation would eventually be resolved in much the same way the Abraham Cohen problem was, but with considerably more success.

Along with thirteen other family-owned stores from across the country, Lazarus helped found the Retail Research Association. The purpose of the RRA was to create a forum for the voluntary exchange of sales and operating figures. This group laid the groundwork for the soon-to-be-formed Associated Merchandising Corporation, which focused on developing merchandising and logistics success factors.

As befitted a modern department store, E.J. Wood, Lazarus display manager, emphasized the importance of color schemes in displaying merchandise to its best advantage. In *Women's Wear* magazine, he asserted, "Color speaks louder than words. It smiles at you or it frowns, as the case may be. It has warmth or it is cold. It is shallow or deep." The store would later refer to such displays as "silent salesmen."

Fred Sr. was known for the pocket watch he carried. It later became a design motif for the store and was the model for the clock on the first floor. When he died in 1917, he was succeeded by his eldest son, Simon, who served for thirty years. Known around the store as "Mr. Si," he enjoyed a reputation as a mild and likable man. Having declared himself "the National Inspector of Jewish Country Clubs," he once played eight of Scotland's best golf courses in ten days. He was also an advocate of minimum wage laws as early as 1914, much to the consternation of many of his fellow merchants.

However, Uncle Si lacked Fred Jr.'s ambition. Even though the new store had been their joint vision, it was Uncle Fred who "went down to New York and arranged for the financing. He arranged the insurance. He let every contract and he personally supervised the construction."

The Bargain Basement was opened in 1917 in what had previously been a stockroom. Filled with manufacturer's closeouts, it was a relatively new concept, and Lazarus was one of the first stores in the country to capitalize on it. Until 1921, a stairwell from High Street just north of the store led directly to what became known as the East Basement.

Initially, there was a stigma attached to the term "basement." However, by the 1920s, most department stores had them, and during the Depression

The Front Street Level as it looked during the 1930s before the ceiling was lowered. *PC.*

store owners saw that even their best customers were sneaking down the stairs in search of a bargain. Nevertheless, management still regarded the basement as the lowest rung on the corporate ladder and often used it as a training ground for buyers, supervisors and others.

During his tenure as a shoe buyer, Tom Eviston witnessed a knock-down, drag-out fight in the basement between two female customers. The shoes had been removed from their boxes, tied together and piled on a table for a big sale. The doors of the store bulged inward as the eager shoppers pressed against them. When they finally were admitted, each woman grabbed one of the shoes and began "socking" the other to make her let go before they were forcibly separated by store associates.

In order to provide a personalized response to questions posed by its mail-order customers, Lazarus created the fictitious "Ann Sterling" as early as 1917.[13] One customer wrote to Ann, "I had three samples of blue velvet and I lost the one I wanted to order, so I am enclosing the other two, and I want two yards of the one different from the two I am sending." An anonymous Lazarus associate ensured that she got it.

The Great War forced the store to close on "Fuel-less Mondays." The Community War Chest, an umbrella organization for local fundraising, was organized by three prominent citizens: Robert Jeffrey of Jeffrey Manufacturing, Robert F. Wolfe of the *Columbus Dispatch* and Simon Lazarus. The forerunner of the United Appeal, Columbus was the first city in the country to have such an agency.

The Front Street Level Children's Shoe Department shortly after it opened. *CCJ.*

Muslin Underwear and Ladies' Sweaters were housed on the third floor. *CML.*

"They all believed that the business would succeed as Columbus succeeded," Charles Lazarus later asserted. "We were all brought up with a theory that you have to give back to the community and you have to build for the community which will assure that we live in a healthy and sound area."

It was during the war that Lazarus introduced the practice of having its staff start out each day with a song to lift morale. Fifty years later, the practice still survived, at least in the warehouse carpeting department, where strains of "I've got that Lazarus feeling down in my heart!" could occasionally be heard early in the morning.

Chapter 6
The Big Circus

A good store is like a big circus," Fred Jr. was often heard to say, and he certainly practiced what he preached. His unique combination of showmanship and clever merchandising boosted not only the store's profits but also its image in the public eye. Years later, Charles Lazarus elaborated on this point:

> *Fifty to one hundred demonstrations should be running continuously; how to brush your hair so that it is curly, how to cook in a chafing dish, how to shampoo rugs. Or maybe there are authors autographing their latest works in the book shop or a marionette show in the children's department. All these things contribute to store excitement and make the customer feel that a visit to the store, even if she has no specific purchase in mind, will be pleasant and rewarding way to spend a few hours of the day.*

"We start with the customers, and the management is at the bottom of the charts," Uncle Fred professed. "Executives are the least important persons; the truly important ones are the customers. They pay our salaries and permit us to do other things that we want done for the business." Every decision was weighed against how it would affect the customers.

When the Armistice Parade passed down High Street in 1918, Lazarus associates abandoned their cash registers and ran out to join the celebration. Bob Sr., home from the war, immediately returned to the store as vice-president, secretary and general manager. Jeffrey, who had also seen military service, resumed his duties as well, although he still was the odd man out.

On Armistice Day 1918, Lazarus associates left their stations and flooded High Street to celebrate. *CML.*

The same year, the Altrusa Club of Columbus was formed at the Southern Hotel. An organization of professional/business women, it was intended to "inspire them to set up high ideals of life and of service to society." The name is a combination of "altruism" and "USA." Mary Love, manager of the Lazarus tearooms, was one of the founders. No less than a dozen other Lazarus associates joined over the years, including Helen Sawyer, Mary Love's successor, and longtime buyer Lola Hasson. Naturally, they had the full support of the store behind them.

A year later, the store employed a nurse for the first time to provide medical aid to its burgeoning number of employees. As early as 1912, some of the larger Boston retailers had begun creating medical departments staffed by a full-time nurse and a part-time doctor. By 1956, it had become such a common occurrence that Helen Wells wrote about it in her young adult novel *Cherry Ames, Department Store Nurse.*

In 1920, with annual sales closing in on the $6 million mark, Lazarus was in competition with the following establishments: Armbruster Company, the Boston Store, John M. Caren & Company, Columbus Dry Goods Company, Nathan Danzinger, the Dunn-Taft Company, the Home Store, John Katz, Miller's Fair, Morehouse-Martens, J.C. Penney and Z.I. White & Company. A number of specialty boutiques were also popping up, such as Mrs. Eugene

Congratulations, little friend,
    And birthday greetings, too:
I'm sixty-nine years old myself,
    But feel as young as you.

The Lazarus Store
— Columbus, Ohio

A 1920 birthday greetings postcard sent to the children of Lazarus customers. *CML*.

Gray, Montaldo's, Pumphrey's and the French Shop.

Printer's Ink, a national trade publication, carried the following "help wanted" ad: "Young woman, Pratt Institute training, department store and agency experience, good in pen and ink or color. References. Moderate salary. Available immediately. Bernice Lunger, care F&R Lazarus & Co., Columbus, Ohio."

Obviously, attitudes had changed since Ralph's day. Female associates were increasingly viewed as critical to the store's success.

The store's first "outside representative" was Chic Harley, the legendary Ohio State football player. He was, undoubtedly, hired for his celebrity value. His heroics on the gridiron inspired the campaign to build Ohio Stadium ("the House that Harley Built"). The fundraising effort kicked off with an ox roast and carnival on October 16, 1920, in honor of the school's fiftieth anniversary. Of course, Lazarus was involved.

Publicity chairman Simon Lazarus ensured that representatives from nearly every Ohio newspaper were on hand by promising a big announcement. They weren't disappointed when a scale model of the sixty-three-thousand-seat stadium, larger than the Coliseum in Rome, was unveiled. The public was asked to pledge $1 million to build the imposing, horseshoe-shaped structure. Simon even persuaded a group of ministers to incorporate the benefits of the stadium into their sermons.

In 1921, just before the stock market took a plunge, F&R Lazarus took a $250,000 markdown on $2.5 million in stock. After clearing the

The ladies' restroom located on the balcony offered plenty of room for resting. *CML.*

The enormous third-floor restroom doubled as a lounge with a bank of pay telephones on the wall. *CML.*

shelves of surplus items, the buyers went back into the distressed market and repurchased merchandise for cash at a discount. It was another bold move, but it paid off within a matter of weeks. While others merchants struggled with excess inventory, Lazarus actually achieved gains in sales.

Soon the company acquired a reputation for performing well even in tough times.

Despite being twice the size of the old one, the new store was already filled to capacity by 1921, so a new $400,000 addition was constructed, increasing floor space by about 40 percent. The High Street entrance was changed to accommodate a lobby lined with thirty-three linear feet of display windows. As the publicity director of Macy's had said, "A window display is a combination of a poster, a newspaper advertisement, a stage set, a speech, and a scarf dance." Certainly, this became true of the famous Lazarus show windows.

To facilitate better traffic flow through the store, three elevators were installed. The Associates' Cafeteria was enlarged, reflecting the increase in the number of employees, as was the men's department, and a gift shop and beauty salon were added. In July 1921, Lazarus held its first Remnant Days sale, a two-day event. It was not unusual to find old coats discarded on the floor as shoppers exchanged them for new ones that they then wore out of the store.

The Shannon Building to the north, housing Times Auto Supply Company, was purchased for use as stock rooms, alteration rooms, advertising department, sign construction, executive offices and the interior decorating department. Only two years later, a fire broke out in the building, destroying many company records, including all advertising files. The alteration rooms

Men's and boys' clothing departments were on the second floor. *CML.*

The Big Circus

The gift shop on the fourth floor offered shoppers a range of impressive, if not particularly practical, items. *CML.*

had to be relocated to "the Barn," as the former livery stable on lower Town Street was known.

The Associate Clinic, which was opened in 1922, three years after the first nurse was hired, was the first of its kind in central Ohio. During the first six months of operation, two nurses made 3,662 home visits to ailing employees. Associates and customers also had access to separate "nap rooms," where they could lie down if they were tired or did not feel well.

Fashion illustrator Karen Ross-Ohlinger recalled, "One artist I knew ate lunch in the cafeteria every day and then after lunch went into the nurse's station to take a short nap on one of their comfy beds! She relied on the nurse to wake her at the appropriate time to return to work."

During the early '20s, the first planned shopping centers began appearing in the United States, but the concept didn't really catch on for many years. Locally, developer Don M. Casto opened the thirty-store Grandview Avenue Shopping Center in 1931. With off-street parking for four hundred cars, Casto's design was widely copied. However, it was no threat to Lazarus.

For the annual store picnic on June 21, 1922, more than seven hundred associates boarded special railroad cars that transported them to the Elmont Hotel in Groveport. There was dinner, dancing and a live radio broadcast from a special station setup on the hotel's porch. They had reason to

Left: Beginning in 1922, Lazarus employed two nurses to make home visits to ailing employees. *PC.*

Below: In 1950, Lazarus recognized that both its customers and its employees sometimes could benefit from a nap. *PC.*

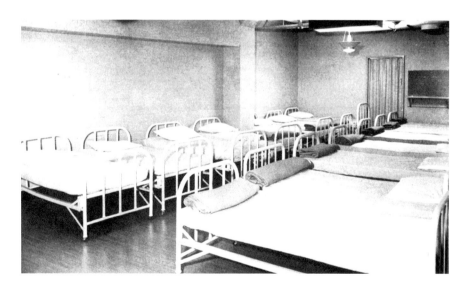

celebrate: their employer treated them well. Already receiving paid holidays, they would soon be given paid sick leave, too.

In 1923, James Thurber, five years out of college (and no longer masquerading as a shoplifter), won first prize in an essay contest sponsored by the F&R Lazarus Store. At the urging of *Columbus Dispatch* literary critic Harold "Cherry" Cherrington, the budding writer was offered a weekly column in the paper entitled "Credos and Curios," providing him with a forum for his literary talents.[14]

A.C. Rundio, well-known Columbus banjo player, was hired by Lazarus to sell musical instruments and Victrola phonographs, earning a mention in a national trade publication. Over the years, many local musicians would follow in his footsteps. Meanwhile, the *Enthusiast* switched from a monthly to a weekly newsletter, and the number of members in the Twenty Year Club reached twenty-three.

On March 23, 1923, amateur actress Agnes Jeffrey Shedd invited five of her friends to a ladies' tea at Lazarus for the purpose of forming a club to stage one-act plays. Calling itself the Players Club, it evolved into the Players Theatre, which was one of the oldest community theater groups in the country before it dissolved in 1993.

In September 1924, the Lazarus University Men's Store opened at 1830 North High Street, between Long's College Book Store and Hennick's Restaurant, famed hangout of Milton Caniff, Elliot Nugent and James Thurber. By 1936, it had disappeared, replaced by a bookstore, the Bibliophile— one of the Lazarus family's rare miscalculations.

During the 1920s, the concept of "dissection control" was adopted. Merchandise departments were split into "customer demand areas" with separate inventory records, sales figures and trend information. Instead of making an associate responsible for the entire toy department, for example, he (or she) might be accountable just for dolls. It wasn't until 1946 that a cash register was purchased that could record sales by dissection— and Toyland got it.

LAZARUS
University Men's
Store Opens

On High Street, at the Campus
A New Idea in Store Service

In 1924, Lazarus opened the University Men's Store on North High Street near Fifteenth Avenue. *PC.*

Still bulging at the seams, Lazarus added the Town and Front building in 1926, replacing the three-story Barn, a four-story warehouse and another three-story structure. It more than doubled the size of the existing store to 417,300 square feet. Some seventy thousand people turned out for the grand opening.

The Roaring Twenties were now in full swing. Dresses were comfortable, skirts short, hair bobbed, undergarments convenient and stockings nude. Bold makeup came into favor. Coco Chanel popularized the cardigan jacket, the little black dress, the wool jersey dress and costume jewelry.

In response, Lazarus opened the Collegienne Shops (renamed Junior Circle in the 1970s), offering coats, suits, dresses, lingerie, shoes and sportswear in junior sizes, reflecting the addition of size and figure specialization in the apparel industry. It had been a long time in coming.

"We were the first store in the country to have true special sizes," said great-grandson Charles Lazarus. "One of the things we did, we went out and researched and found that there was a big difference in the hips, the waist, above the waist and the bust. We got people to manufacture according to our specifications for those sizes. We bought out the market because there wasn't anybody that made those sizes."

All existing departments were once again remodeled, with the following additions: furniture, rugs and carpet, draperies and curtains, interior

When Lazarus opened the Collegienne Shop in the mid-1920s, it was one of the first stores in the country to offer special sizes. *PC.*

decorating services, housewares/china/glass, radios and record players, appliances, the Pavilion Tea Room (added to Main Dining Room on fifth floor) and the Colonial Room (which replaced the Balcony Tea Room).

It had been seventy-five years since the opening of the original B. Aronson & Brother. To celebrate the "Diamond Jubilee," a New Year's Eve street party took place at the corner of Town and High, with music provided by the Franklin Post American Legion Band. Sixteen associates dressed as clowns handed out candy, while twenty-two young girls posted on the store's marquee rained serpentine ribbons and confetti down on the crowd of ten thousand.

Governor Vic Donahey, the foremost vote-getter of his day, and the Diamond Jubilee Quartet were heard via a live radio broadcast. The

This conceptual sketch for the unpublished history of Lazarus was rejected because of the drunk in the foreground. *EH*.

Tab Kirk, a Lazarus associate, models the actual Miss America robe for the Diamond Jubilee in 1926. *PC.*

quartet also sang with the Lazarus Entertainers, all store associates, who performed throughout the store. One female associate, Tab Kirk, was selected to model the actual ermine and velvet Miss America robe, valued at $15,000.

An "Old Folks Party" for customers seventy-five years or older was held for the first time in 1926 (a year earlier, a special "tea" had been staged for women seventy years or older). Because it took place during the anniversary month of March, someone decided to use pastel green icing on the cake because of the event's proximity to St. Patrick's Day. Few pieces were consumed, however, due to an old (and not entirely unfounded) fear of arsenic in green food coloring.

Another year was added each year thereafter to keep pace with the age of the store until it was capped at eighty and renamed the "Eighty Year Old Party." For several years after World War II, the event was held outside the store because the Lazarus Assembly Center couldn't accommodate the crowds. But after the guests expressed their displeasure with this arrangement—they wanted to go shopping!—the event was broken down into a series of parties, each hosting from four to five hundred guests.

Later in 1926, the first Fall Style Evening debuted. The store closed at 5:30 p.m. so that associates could rush home to dress up. It then reopened from 7:00 p.m. to 10:00 p.m. However, no selling took place. Instead, customers were invited to attend a party with live music and vaudeville performances on each floor. There were special displays, demonstrations, book signings and so on, and the third-floor style shows took place on specially constructed ramps down the main aisle. Tens of thousands of people showed up for this annual event. In 1934, though, it was discontinued because of the impact of the Great Depression on retail sales.

For many years (1926–39), the book department at Lazarus on the Front Street Level was presided over by Lulu S. Teeter, a nationally respected figure in the world of publishing whose passing ("the late and deeply loved") was noted in *Saturday Review* magazine. Under her guidance, it became a center of literary affairs in Ohio. Lulu discussed literature on her regular radio broadcasts, initiated a direct mail program "to reach the neglected farm market," championed children's books and earned the gratitude of many authors.

By 1927, Lazarus had 1,500 associates, ten times what it had less than thirty years before. That number would double over the next twenty years. Perhaps even more significantly, the first associate retired and began drawing a pension.

For the store's seventy-sixth anniversary, "Our Creed" was published in the *Enthusiast*:

> *I believe in the Lazarus Store because it is founded on right principles and aims at the highest ideals.*

In 1929, the Book Department was run by Lulu S. Teeter, a nationally respected figure in the publishing world. *CML.*

I believe in that diligent service to the public for which the name Lazarus stands: in earnest devotion to the best interests of its customers.

I believe in the men and women associated here, helping to build, with energy and enthusiasm, one of the great stores of America.

So I highly resolve to work with head and heart and hand to do my part worthily, in the spirit of this institution, striving to make it proud of me as I am proud of it.

While the *Enthusiast* was a publication by and for the store's employees and not a platform for management, the creed accurately reflects the feelings of many former Lazarus associates to this day. It was always more than a job.

Ever on the lookout for new worlds to conquer, Fred Jr. embarked on a new adventure in 1928 when Lazarus bought John Shillito's in Cincinnati for $2.5 million. The oldest department store west of the Alleghenies, Shillito's had been the city's largest retail merchant until 1925, when it dropped to fourth. At the time, the downtown store had featured a six-story atrium with a magnificent hexagonal glass dome sixty feet in diameter. However, the Cincinnati Fire Department would soon insist that it be boarded over for safety reasons.

According to Charlotte Witkind, "Uncle Si, Uncle Fred, and Dad [Robert Sr.] were all crazy about each other," but "Uncle Jack [Jeffrey] used to drive the others nuts. He was the youngest, and he was bullheaded as hell." By acquiring Shillito's, Uncle Fred had a means of getting Jeffrey out of everyone's hair by exiling him to Cincinnati.

After the purchase, Fred Jr. completely refurbished the store and infused it with his own management ideas. With Uncle Jack as general manager (and, later, president), assisted by various Lazarus buyers, management and other key personnel who made the two-hundred-mile round-trip drive two or three days a week, the store was soon able to stand on its own. Within a year, sales had grown to $5.7 million, and by 1939, the Lazarus-owned and Lazarus-operated Shillito's was once again the top store in its market.

"The customer must be satisfied with the goods," Fred Jr. always maintained. "That comes first." Regarded as a great showman and one of the most dynamic figures in department store history, Uncle Fred seemingly had his fingers in everything. It was he who bought the alligator that was a popular attraction in the store's basement for eighteen years. It was he who hired a blimp to announce a change in store hours. He also started the annual Santa Claus parade, the practice of giving free saplings to schoolchildren on Arbor Day and fashion shows at stockholders meetings.

Although a giant in his field, Fred was not much over five feet tall. He suffered from tremors throughout his entire life and could barely manage to sign his name. While attending an ROTC class in 1902, he shot out a light bulb in the armory ceiling because he could not hold the gun steady. And his driving was so bad that few dared to ride with him.

Uncle Fred seemed to be in perpetual, if erratic, motion. As younger brother, Bob, put it, "I've only envied Fred one thing, and that's been his drive and his terrific nervous energy. Many's the time I've said to him, 'Fred, you need a vacation. I'm awfully tired.'"

For the second annual fall style show in September 1928, an estimated twenty-five thousand people turned out. Every floor of the store was crowded with people eager to see what well-dressed women and men would be wearing that season. The display department had arranged merchandise in forty-seven windows. Lazarus served up seven separate style shows, featuring 130 living models (including 14 children ages two to fourteen) and seven orchestras, supplemented by a miniature radio broadcasting station and numerous phonographs.

There was also a model house; a new, wood-paneled beauty salon; and a viewing station for home movies, as well as waffles, coffee and toast served up by the associates in Kitchenware. One year, Katrina Van Televox, a "female" robot that obeyed spoken commands, was the star for the fall spectacular, attracting fifty thousand visitors in a single day.

Lazarus was always thinking outside the box. When the brothers wanted to increase sales in yard goods and patterns, they hit on the novel idea of turning all of the silk department salesgirls into customers so that they could experience firsthand what it was like to shop at Lazarus. And since it was a training exercise, the company paid for it all.

Chapter 7

A Few-Pennies-a-Day

T he year 1929 was an especially momentous one in the history of the United States. Seven Chicago gangsters were gunned down in the St. Valentine's Day Massacre, Herbert Hoover succeeded Calvin Coolidge as president, *Amos 'n' Andy* debuted on NBC radio and Admiral Byrd flew over the South Pole. However, the most pivotal event occurred on October 24, "Black Thursday," when the bottom dropped out of the U.S. stock market, ushering in the twelve-year-long Great Depression.

According to economist Richard M. Salsman, "Anyone who bought stocks in mid-1929 and held onto them saw most of his or her adult life pass by before getting back to even." Although the F&R Lazarus & Company finished the year with $12,875,000 in sales, hard times lay ahead. During the next five years, total retail sales nationwide would drop to half of what they had been.

Earlier in the year, Fred Jr.'s son had been run down by an automobile. While still grieving the boy's death, Fred was instrumental in devising a plan that would help protect Lazarus (and Shillito's) from incurring major losses during the Depression by joining with Abraham & Straus of Brooklyn and William Filene's Sons of Boston in a holding company.

The partnership, incorporated as Federated Department Stores, enabled the owners to pool their risks since they were now shareholders in the larger enterprise rather than their individual stores. On September 25, 1929, Bloomingdale Brothers of New York City threw in its lot with these other merchant princes. During the year, aggregate sales for the four stores exceeded $100 million. (See Appendix I.)

The Lazarus Charm House was a popular place to visit on the fourth floor. *CML.*

Lazarus was quickly becoming known for its practice of hiring women, as well as the physically challenged. One of these women was Bella Cabakoff, a Russian emigrant, who at age twenty-one became the store's youngest buyer. She joined the staff not long after the stock market crash and remained for more than twenty years.

Finally, in 1951, Bella left Lazarus and with her husband, Harry Wexner, opened a woman's clothing store on State Street. They called it Leslie's in honor of their son, who worked in it briefly after dropping out of law school. However, in 1963, young Les Wexner started a store of his own, the Limited, at Kingsdale Shopping Center and transformed it into a multibillion-dollar clothing empire. The Limited was, in a sense, the anti-Lazarus because Les chose to focus on just one particular market segment—younger women.

Not long after Bella was hired, Eileen Heckart, a Bexley native, gave the first of many legendary performances by throwing a tantrum in the ladies' department. Dropping to the floor, twelve-year-old Eileen transformed herself into a ball of fury, kicking and screaming until her grandmother agreed to buy her a hat. Once outside, her grandmother also gave her a punch in the mouth.[15] Forty years later, Eileen would win a best supporting actress Oscar for *Butterflies Are Free.*

Since its inception five years earlier, the Fall Style Evening had developed into such an enormous undertaking that in 1931 Lazarus and the Union

Give the Loveliness of

Glove-Silk Vests, Bloomers, Panties

Priced Extra-Special

$1.79

This is no ordinary lingerie . . . but perfect dreams of gifts! Brief little panties and bloomers delicate with lace . . . vests that fit sleekly as couturier frocks! And in every instance, the enchanting lure of flower-colors . . . irresistibly desirable!

First Floor

LAZARUS

This 1930 lingerie ad shows how dramatically fashions had changed after the Great War. *PC.*

jointly sponsored the event. Although they were, technically, competitors, the Union actually specialized in higher-end ("carriage trade") clothing and was not a full-line department store. This mutually beneficial arrangement continued for three more years.

Throughout the 1930s, Lazarus made every effort to hang on to its veteran staff, in spite of a dramatic drop in sales. Various cost-saving measures were put in place to hold down expenses—and prices—without sacrificing customer service. For example, the *Enthusiast* was discontinued for three years. It was resumed in 1933.

Women's fashions were changing, too, in response to the flagging economy. The ninety-nine-cent house dress—a simple shift with a tie belt and short kimono sleeves—became the de facto uniform of the housewife. There was even greater emphasis on separates (jackets, sweaters and skirts) that could be combined into multiple outfits in order to increase a woman's wardrobe options.

When President Franklin Delano Roosevelt declared a national bank holiday on March 4, 1933, Lazarus took advantage of this opportunity to begin promoting its own charge accounts. Within a year, it would also create the Lazarus Credit Union (which replaced the Lazarus Savings Association), providing its associates with a more favorable way of saving and borrowing than the local banks could offer.

While the national retail media debated the pros and cons, Lazarus experimented with arranging merchandise by size. Fred Jr. had first seen this in practice while visiting the Prisunic store on the Champs-Élysées in Paris. Historically, items had been arranged strictly by brand and price, the way inventory was kept. Retailers had feared that grouping by size would encourage customers to buy the cheapest item, but this did not prove to be the case.

Lazarus also began open stock selling. Instead of storing merchandise in drawers, on shelves or behind glass display counters, where sales associates had to fetch it, everything was made readily accessible to customers. Naturally, fewer employees were required to support a self-service sales model, further reducing costs.

In 1934, Lazarus became one of the first major stores in the country to air-condition its selling floors. Water was obtained from a well sunk at Town and Front Streets. Unfortunately, the water's high sulfur content gave it a terrible odor. Whenever the air-conditioning system sprung a leak, fumes

The hat shop as it looked in the early 1930s before Lazarus began experimenting with open stock selling. *PC.*

would turn all of the silver in the store black, including the doorknobs. After the water was used for cooling, it could not be dumped into the nearby Scioto River, so it was drained back into another well.

On March 2, Francis Schmidt, Ohio State's newly hired football coach, was asked by reporters to comment on how he would deal with their archrivals, the Michigan Wolverines. "They put on their pants one leg at a time, the same as we do," he replied. When the Buckeyes went on to beat Michigan 34–0, Simon Lazarus and Herbert Levy (president of the Union) gave the players a gold charm depicting a pair of football pants, initiating a tradition that has continued ever since.

Among Lazarus's competitors during the mid-1930s were such prominent High Street retailers as the Union, the Boston Store, Dunn-Taft, the Fashion, Morehouse-Martens and Moby's. Two others, Danzinger's and the Climax, were located over on Mount Vernon Avenue, while Schottenstein's was way down south at 1887 Parsons Avenue. However, it was quickly boiling down to F&R Lazarus and everybody else.

In response to the Federal Housing Act of 1934, which authorized loans for home modernization, Lazarus created the "Few-Pennies-A-Day" program. Originally, the no–down payment plan was limited to such goods as carpet, floor tile and water heaters—items that became a semipermanent part of the home.

Sponsored by Lazarus, Montana Meechy and his Cowboy Band were heard regularly on WAIU radio. *PC.*

A Few-Pennies-a-Day

"We already have a deferred payment plan with a 20% down payment," Robert Lazarus declared. "If we are willing to trust customers for 80% of the purchase, why not 100%?" By 1936, the program was extended to all big-ticket hard goods and some soft goods as well.

Lazarus also initiated the Good Business Bonus as a way of rewarding associates who demonstrated high levels of customer service. Adam Smith had discussed the topic as far back as 1778 in *The Wealth of Nations*, but the Lazarus family seems to have had an intuitive grasp of the fact that unless they met their customers' needs, they would go elsewhere.

"I'll never forget the first sale I had," Mr. Charles once said. He was working in piece goods at the time. "We were having a sale at nine cents a yard of percale strips to make a patchwork quilt. I spent the next two hours cutting those strips for a total sale that amounted to about thirty or forty cents. That was my introduction to patience with customers and service in retail."

As a further means of keeping workers happy and productive, the Lazarus Athletic Association (LAA) was formed. Evolving out of the bowling league, this employee-run organization provided associates with all manner of social activities, including tennis, bowling nights, a baseball league, a theatrical society and a choral group, as well as bridge, rifle, book, photography, swimming and glee clubs.

Tom Eviston once ran for LAA presidency. He headed the winning ticket when the Surazal ("Lazarus" spelled backward) Rebels were pitted against the Yankee Hi-Towners (High and Town Streets). For three days, they campaigned during the hour before the store opened each morning.

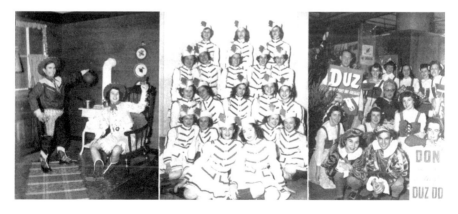

Just a sampling of what Lazarus associates were up to in 1950 as members of the Lazarus Athletic Association. *PC.*

The "Surazal Party" headed one ticket in the Lazarus Athletic Association leadership election. *TE.*

The "Hi-Towners" were the rival LAA party during the 1960s. *TE.*

A Few-Pennies-a-Day

After the results of the election were in, everyone celebrated at the Great Southern Hotel (once co-owned by Ralph Lazarus). *TE.*

Afterward, they celebrated their victory at the Great Southern Hotel. Such activities helped to build the associates' sense of camaraderie.

There are innumerable stories regarding the store's no-questions-asked return policy; everyone who ever worked there has at least one. Mr. Charles related one when he was a buyer of ladies fur coats:

> *We used to run these $38 fur sales…and for every sale, we'd find two or three minks in the stock and mix them in with the rabbits and God knows what else. I remember being on the floor one day…when a lady came into the store screaming. She tried to convince us that the skins weren't dead and they smelled to high-heaven. We gave her back her money and sent her on her way.*

When she became divisional director of customer service, Sue Robenalt was told to do whatever it took to resolve a complaint. By the time a disgruntled customer reached her office, they were often extremely upset. She was regularly subjected to crying, screaming and heavy doses of profanity. The first order of business was simply to calm the person down and get his or her attention.

The weirdest complaint Sue ever handled involved an electric blanket that had shorted out and caught fire because a child had wet it while sleeping. Although the tag clearly stated the blanket was not for use with young children, Lazarus paid for the child's medical bills, damaged furniture and bedding and even threw in an assortment of toys because "the customer is always right."

Lazarus had opened a Trade-In Furniture Store when it became apparent that there was a growing market for used furniture. Then, as the country slowly emerged from the Depression in 1939, the company ramped up its hiring in preparation for the opening of the Lazarus Service Building at the southeast corner of State and Front Streets. This ten-story edifice, which occupied the site of the trade-in store, added 385,000 more square feet.

Initially, only the Front Street Level was used for selling. The building's purpose was to provide horizontal (or "direct") warehousing; the reserve stock for each department was housed in immediate proximity to the selling floor. The result was decreased handling costs and increased speed and efficiency.

Other changes included the addition of musical instruments, musical instruction studios, a bake shop and the Rose Fountain Restaurant. Housewares, china, glass, appliances, radios, cameras, sporting goods and luggage were expanded on both Front Street Levels (North and South), while more space was freed up on the third floor for the Collegienne Shops.

An Assembly Center was constructed on the Front Street Level North, while the accounting department was enlarged and updated. The emphasis on leisure and hobby goods paralleled the country's shift to shorter workdays. Someone commented in 1940 that Simon Lazarus's original store would have fit inside the umbrella department on the main floor of the High Street addition.

For the building's opening festivities, an amazing new invention was demonstrated: television. However, nothing more came of it for about ten years due to the intrusion of World War II. Instead, the crowds were more enthused about the clothes sloshing about in the first Bendix automatic washing machines. Electric refrigerators, washers and radios had also entered into mass production.

In an interview with fashion writer Marshall Hood, Lola Hasson remembered that "even as a child, my mother made us wear hats and gloves when we came into town." Later as a coed at Ohio State University, "We wore sweaters and skirts and black-and-white saddle shoes." When she was hired at Lazarus in 1937, it was with the expectation that she would look the part. "In the beginning, we were not allowed to go to New York on buying trips without a hat. Robert Lazarus Sr. expected everybody to look nice."

After three months on the job, Lola was invited to meet with Uncle Si in his private office, as was customary with all new employees. He asked her if she was happy with her job and then offered her the following advice: "Think like a man, act like a lady, work like a dog."

According to Harriet Bracken, one-time editor of the *Enthusiast*, after these initial meetings Uncle Si would always address the associate by name from then on. During the war, copies of the company newsletter were sent to all Lazarus men and women serving in the military, along with a Christmas package. "The relationship of caring, concern and loyalty, in reality, might be gone forever," Harriet lamented, "but its impact on our working lives was significant."

Aspiring actress Eileen Heckart returned to Lazarus while working her way through college:[16]

> *They put me in what was called the hot-items section. They had a special sale on hot items every day. I was good at selling very fast, very persuasive, very sure of myself…I gave makeup demonstrations for Max Factor cosmetics, and meanwhile I did commercials for local radio stations and, eventually, did drama in radio. I booked fashion shows into sorority houses and distributed samples of Philip Morris cigarettes to the other kids.*

Many years afterward, Bob Sr. told the *Columbus Citizen-Journal* that the economic recovery was slower in Columbus than it should have been because of the city's "insular attitude." He specifically blamed the chamber of commerce, which was reluctant to pursue heavy industry, fearing that it would also bring unions.

Both the American Federation of Labor (1886) and the United Mine Workers of America (1890) had been founded in Columbus, but it wasn't until the 1930s that there was significant growth in Ohio's labor unions. In Akron and Youngstown, the rubber workers and the steelworkers soon won the right to bargain collectively. By 1939, roughly 25 percent of the state's nonfarm employees had joined unions. City fathers were, apparently, determined not to let it happen here.

For its part, Lazarus launched a series of educational meetings for managers, designed to help them understand the profit objective of each department. Because the store was ahead of the curve when it came to collecting and analyzing data on all aspects of retailing, most of its training programs were by necessity developed in-house. Sue Robenalt felt that was its strength.

Starting on May 23, 1942, Lazarus promoted the selling of war bonds in its corner window at High and Town Streets. A special door was constructed to allow direct entry from the street. Dubbed "Victory Corner," it was staffed by two full-time associates who were dedicated to the task of selling war bonds and stamps to the citizens of Columbus. They were frequently joined by local and national celebrities such as Marlene Dietrich. In all, Victory Corner raised $17,360,750 for the war effort.

Meanwhile, the Lazarus Store Foundation developed a plan to provide emergency financial aid to needy associates. From management's standpoint, they were all in this together. Rationing of shoes and restaurant foods, price controls and grave shortages of consumer goods continued to take a toll on sales. Buyers frantically searched for merchandise to sell, while customers frantically searched for merchandise to buy.

Austerity measures put into place during World War II directly affected clothing design. Hems could be no more than two inches deep, trouser cuffs were forbidden and a blouse could only have one pocket. Simplification and streamlining was the order of the day.

As the men went off to war, jobs were shuffled and women had to increasingly step into traditionally male positions. In 1942, Betty Anderson Newell became one of the first women to work in small package delivery. She had seen a notice posted on the bulletin board and applied for the job along with a friend. Betty particularly enjoyed driving the truck. She recalled that they would deliver everything from a spool of thread to items weighing thirty pounds.

For wartime homemakers, Lazarus offered classes in cooking, sewing and nursing as a public service. It also served as a collection station for discarded nylon, rayon and silk hosiery, as well as old furs—all of which were needed for the war effort. The store ran ads encouraging citizens to carpool because "Empty seats are Sabotage!" (See Appendix III.)

In the mid-1940s, Lazarus held its first major color promotion in fashion, "Wild Rose." For the next fifteen years, the store held a major color promotion in February and another in August for one-color women's outfits. It was not a "sale" because Washington banned the use of the word in 1943, an unnecessary exercise in governmental meddling given that demand for most goods far exceeded supply.

The celebrated F&R Lazarus Record Library was opened in 1944, promising "Every Record at Your Fingertips." There were eighteen soundproof listening booths so customers could sample a recording before they bought it. Six of the booths were dedicated specifically for classical recordings.

"Make it easy for 'em, make it interesting for 'em and they'll buy is the proved sales psychology behind the self-service boom," a contemporary article declared. Actually, the record department was never more than a break-even proposition. (Although, when Elvis died in 1977, the department

The basement Hosiery Department was strictly hands-off before World War II. *PC.*

supervisor estimated that he sold $50,000 worth of Elvis material in a little more than two hours!) Lazarus simply did not want to give a customer reason to go looking elsewhere.

The Lazarus budget charge account with revolving credit service was introduced in 1945. Through extensive promotion, Lazarus had soon issued more cards than any other store in the country. Five years later, there would be more than fifty thousand accounts outside Franklin County. The success of this program necessitated the expansion of the accounting department, which was relocated to the fourth floor in 1948.

Also in 1945, Fred Jr. took charge of Federated Department Stores, replacing the company's first president, Lincoln Filene (who became chairman). After creating new divisions in finance, research and development, operations and acquisitions, the company began aggressively acquiring other department stores across the United States. "After sixteen years of dormancy," Jonathan Schwartz noted, "Federated finally sprang to life with the purchase of Houston based Foley's."

According to Charles, "Uncle Fred had moved to Cincinnati to set up a central headquarters for Federated because he felt that Federated and Lazarus were making all the money and they were 'milking' us. So he decided there had to be a central management, and he set up a financial and legal real estate management." Maybe. But not all members of the family saw it that way.

Chapter 8

The Temple of Commerce

With the war at an end, thousands of GIs were coming home, taking jobs, getting married, starting families, entering college and buying homes. In response, Lazarus hired a personnel counselor to assist its associates in dealing with various problems, both work-related and otherwise. There were adjustments to be made by returning servicemen and the women who, in their absence, had been forced to become more independent. Some things would never go back to the way they were.

As early as 1916, George F. Johnson had implemented a forty-hour workweek in his Endicott-Johnson factories, but it wasn't until after World War II that it became common in most industries. Lazarus introduced the forty-hour work week in 1946. At the same time, associates with ten years of seniority were granted three weeks of paid vacation; with twenty years of seniority, two summer weeks and two winter weeks; and all others, two weeks.

Although shopping centers began springing up in the early 1920s, Lazarus continued to believe that it would be more prudent to further develop and reinvent the downtown store rather than build suburban locations. Over a period of fifteen years, ending in 1961, the company spent more than $12 million in an effort to ensure that shoppers would still find shopping downtown an attractive proposition.

It began with the purchase of the old Columbus Auditorium, located diagonally across the street from the main store at 199 South Front Street on the southwest corner of Front and Town. Originally built in 1927 as a venue for plays, wrestling matches, basketball games, marathon dances and other exhibitions, it was easily converted into a retail space. After pouring a

The Columbus Auditorium was purchased by Lazarus and opened as the annex in 1946. *CML.*

concrete floor at the balcony level, the building was reopened in 1946 as the Lazarus Annex.

The upper floor, which included a gymnasium with basketball hoops, was used for reserve stock, while the main floor offered washers, dryers, refrigerators and other appliances, lawn mowers, electric kitchen appliances, auto supplies, cookware and other housewares, all relocated from across the street. At some point, a tunnel was constructed, running beneath Front Street to the main store and accessed via a ladder.

Despite concerns that customers would not cross the street, the Lazarus Annex was an immediate success. Among its initial offerings were fireplace fixtures, unpainted furniture, housewares, home appliances, a garden center and other items calculated to appeal to the suburban shopper. Although the annex served the store well for many years, it eventually outlived its usefulness and was demolished on November 11, 1992.

The opening of the annex allowed the basement store to spread into the vacated Front Street Level South and part of the Front Street Level North. Sporting goods, luggage, radios, stereos and cameras were enlarged. The second floor, previously home to the children's departments, was converted to a series of ladies' budget apparel shops and expanded men's clothing departments.

In January 1947, Lustron Corporation, on the strength of a $12.5 million Reconstruction Finance Corporation loan, announced its intention to mass-produce prefabricated houses out of enamel-coated steel panels of the type commonly used for gas stations and White Castle restaurants. One of the company's partners was F&R Lazarus & Company, which offered furniture groupings designed specifically for the homes. "Lustron Built it…Lazarus Furnished it!"

Manufactured in Columbus at the former Curtiss-Wright aircraft plant, Lustron Homes were originally targeted at returning GIs. Although they would "defy weather, wear, and time," the houses proved to be too expensive for most buyers, and by 1950 the company was bankrupt.

Also in 1947, Lazarus associates were provided access to an in-house doctor. The following year, they received hospitalization and surgical coverage through the Lazarus Assurance Plan. Employees were also encouraged to share their own ideas for improvements through "Suggest-a-Plan." One such suggestion gave them their birthdays off as a paid holiday.

When he was attending Ohio State on the GI Bill, Jack Buck used to host a Saturday morning big-band program at Lazarus. Broadcasting over WCOL radio, he would begin each show with, "Hello ladies and gentlemen from Lazarus Department Store in downtown Columbus, Ohio. Lazarus presents the music of Glen Gray and his Rippling Rhythm Review."[17] Jack would later become the longtime voice of the St. Louis Cardinals.

Simon Lazarus, son of Fred Sr., passed away in 1947, having served as president of the store for thirty years. A rather retiring figure, Uncle Si was remembered for his smile and the white carnation he always wore in his lapel. In his memory, the white carnation became the emblem of the Twenty Year Club. The store now had some 3,000 associates. Of the 285 executives in the company, 274 had risen through the ranks from nonexecutive positions.

Robert Lazarus Sr. then took the helm, while Charles (son of Simon) and Ralph (son of Fred Jr.) were named executive vice-presidents. This arrangement continued for three years until Uncle Bob fell ill. In about 1951 or 1952, Uncle Ralph joined his father in Cincinnati. Charles was asked to relocate, too, but did not want to leave his hometown. He remained behind as the sole executive vice-president.

Postwar fashions were in stark contrast to the narrow, skimpy, sheathlike outfits that had been in vogue during the conflict. Christian Dior introduced the "New Look," which was a throwback to the Victorian era with nipped-in waists, fitted bodices and soft, longer skirts. Other designers followed his lead.

"Retailing is an unnerving business," a competitor observed. "But whatever has to be done tomorrow, that Lazarus outfit will have already done it." Although Lazarus was "the Temple of Commerce in Columbus,

Left to right: Ralph, Robert Sr. and Charles Lazarus in 1950, planning for the future. *PC.*

Ohio" (to quote Stephen Miller of the *Wall Street Journal*), the High Street area "was resplendent with small specialty stores" (women's and men's clothing, jewelry, luggage, furniture and more) and "larger stores providing a wider range of goods" (Moby's, J.C. Penney, the Boston Store, the Union and Morehouse-Fashion).

Beginning in 1947, the Lazarus Customer Preference training program was implemented. The intent was to formalize attitudes natural to successful and experienced sales staff so that the young associates could become effective more quickly. A year later, Red Apple pins were introduced, recognizing associates who had been nominated by customers for their courtesy. Those who earned five Red Apples received a bronze pin, while two bronzes equaled a silver and two silvers a gold. These pins quickly became badges of honor among the Lazarus employees and never failed to attract the attention of customers.

The first experiment with a moving staircase[18] had been an unmitigated failure, but in 1948 Lazarus installed a new model from the Front Street Level to the sixth floor. Because the store grew organically, the Front Street Level was below the basement, prompting a sign above the escalator that read, "Up To Basement." Formerly a stockroom, the sixth floor was converted to a sales floor with a progression of boys' and girls' shops (infants to teens), a maternity apparel shop and Toyland. It also housed a new Assembly Center for holding special events.

During the late 1940s, the F&R Lazarus & Company sponsored a half-hour radio program on WCOL that featured a dramatic account of the founding of the Columbus Philharmonic. Conductor Izler Solomon, who would be acclaimed for his work with the Indianapolis Symphony, performed on the broadcast and concluded by thanking the people of Columbus for their support. Members of the Lazarus family had been behind the orchestra from its inception.

A Fall Sale was added to the Lazarus calendar in November (and later moved to October). In retailing circles, the store had already developed a reputation for its January and July Remnant Day sales in which items were marked down. Toward the end of the decade, it added preseason February and August sales for new fashions, which included style shows, puppet shows (to keep the kids occupied) and other entertainments. Import Fairs, usually held in October, were introduced during this period and continued to be held until 1973.

In 1949, the first Bulk Storage Building was opened at 562 Whittier Street, less than a mile southwest of the store. It replaced four ramshackle warehouses. The 265,000-square-feet structure received national attention as the first retail service building to employ industrial factory techniques for handling bulk goods. Instead of being multistoried, it was a broad, one-story affair allowing for the use of forklifts, dollies, floats (four-wheeled carts) and other labor-saving devices. It also freed up 30,000 square feet at the main store, which permitted the expansion of the sales floor.

Up until then, Lazarus operated its stockrooms in the conventional manner (i.e., merchandise was crammed into whatever space was available). However, with the opening of a new retail warehouse, store management decided to take a scientific approach. Not only did it prove to be faster and cheaper (cutting 25 percent off the cost of handling heavy merchandise), "It delivers the goods as slickly and quickly as a penny vending machine," according to an article in *Changing Times*.

One of the workers in the new warehouse was young Alfred W. Harmon. Several years after his widowed mother, Amy, married Uncle Si in 1940, he took a job at Lazarus. He quickly found his niche in retailing, rising to the position of assistant buyer in charge of mattresses. After going on to serve

The new Lingerie Department as it appeared in 1949. *CCJ.*

as an executive with the Cleveland-based Ohio Mattress Company (which became Sealy, Inc.), he purchased the Original Mattress Factory and gained a measure of fame as its TV spokesperson.

In a career that spanned forty-one years, Leonard Daloia has just one regret: he didn't go to college. However, he quickly adds that Lazarus *was* his college: "If they felt you had talent, they developed you"—which is how a vocational sales student from Central High School wound up as vice-president of promotions.

Not long after he was hired on as a copywriter, Leonard was approached by Tom Stimmel, who wanted to take out a full-page ad to promote a shirt sale. Although they were Arrow shirts, they were irregulars and the labels had been removed, so the brand could not be mentioned. Since his boss was unavailable, Leonard took it upon himself to write the following headline: "We can't tell you the famous name, but it rhymes with 'sparrow.'" Although he fully expected to get fired for his cheekiness, Leonard found instead that he had gained their admiration for his creativity.

When buyer Lola Hasson came to Leonard, she was discouraged. After *Life* magazine ran a photo of actress Rita Hayworth in a white flowing dress (with her new husband, Prince Ally Khan), she had stocked a large quantity of them, thinking that they would fly off the racks. But the store hadn't sold a one. So Leonard decided to run the ad again, but with a new headline: "This dress is making history on the Riviera." Suddenly they couldn't keep them in stock.

Because fashions for adolescents were not widely available in many communities, Lazarus began advertising in magazines geared specifically for teenagers. A single ad for a $13.99 dress generated a phenomenal thirteen thousand orders in 1946, supporting Leonard's belief that people believe what they read in headlines.

From the late '40s and into the early '50s, the exterior of the store was renovated with the application of a marble façade on the side facing High Street. The sales floor was deepened through the elimination of the window-lined High Street lobby, and a lighted sign was installed on the High/Town corner. Since windows were no longer needed for lighting, those on Town, Front and State Streets were sealed to improve heating and cooling.

Other changes included the construction of a new Associate Center on the second floor of the State Street Building, an expanded Associates' Cafeteria and the creation of a general commissary for all restaurants adjacent to the cafeteria kitchen. A clinic, a personnel training office, an executive conference room and a credit union were also built.

By hiring minority sales associates, Lazarus was in the forefront of advancing the cause of civil rights. In fact, when it came time for Leonard Daloia to retire after forty-one years, he had to call on one of the early black employees to "certify" that he was working at the store during a period when the records were incomplete. Iris Cooper, who joined Lazarus in 1977, marveled at how many African Americans held management positions in the organization, including James Robinson, head of Human Resources.

At mid-century, Lazarus occupied a unique position as the only full-line department store in Columbus, "offering everything from furniture, household appliances, and auto equipment to clothing for both sexes of all ages and income levels." Although the city could boast 133 department stores and specialty clothing shops, none could approach Lazarus in terms of physical size and breadth of merchandise and services. It was a rare central Ohioan who did not shop there.

Meanwhile, on the far east side, the ribbon was cut on another Don Casto development, Town & Country Shopping Center. Located on a

The new parking garage on Town Street won a major architecture award in 1949. *CCJ.*

45.7-acre tract in suburban Whitehall, it is regarded as one of the first modern shopping centers in the United States, especially when compared to his original Grandview Heights design. At the time, there were fewer than one hundred shopping centers nationwide. Lazarus executives closely watched this development but resisted the pressure to join in the migration to the suburbs.

Instead, Lazarus concentrated on providing low-cost parking, particularly for women, who were only now starting to get behind the wheel. With this in mind, the company opened the first of what was to become four downtown garages, winning an award from Ohio architects. Traffic engineers praised it as a "nearly ideal" terminal since it was only two blocks off High Street and one block away from the main store. Management's goal was to do whatever was necessary to keep the shoppers coming downtown.

Chapter 9

Look to Lazarus

In 1921, cartoonist William "Billy" Ireland of the *Columbus Dispatch* suggested that Fred Lazarus Jr. might "forget" the store's 100th anniversary—which wouldn't occur for thirty more years! The joke was that "Junior" (as competitors called him behind his back) *never* missed an opportunity to talk about Lazarus. But when the time rolled around, he had other things on his mind besides celebrating the longevity of the family business.

On the heels of Macy's acquisition of San Francisco–based O'Connor-Moffat in 1948, Uncle Fred had said, "Hardly a major U.S. store is now run by men who bear the store's name." He would know. The retail world was changing, and perhaps as much as anyone (and more than most), he was changing it.

In 1950, there were four thousand department stores, more or less, nationwide. Of these, an estimated three hundred were responsible for 75 percent or more of all department store sales. And of these, about seventy-five dominated the marketplace—none more so than Lazarus. It was the one store all the others wanted to be.

Despite a lackluster economy, the April 9, 1951 issue of *Newsweek* reported that "Lazarus enjoys 60 per cent of the department-store business in its trading area, and 11 per center of all retail sales." No retailer before or since has been so enmeshed in the daily life of a community.

Ever since replacing Lincoln Filene, Fred Jr. had been doing what he could to ensure that Federated Department Stores did not become the millstone around the Lazarus store's neck. He clearly believed that there was safety in numbers. Once he starting buying up other department stores, he didn't intend to stop until he had put together the largest retail conglomerate in the nation.

Back in Columbus, Robert Sr. had a more modest objective: to protect and expand Lazarus's hold on the central Ohio market.

In 1950, the Lazarus Self-Improvement Clinics for teens and "twixteens" were introduced to teach young girls self-confidence: how to walk on a style-show runway, how to sit down and how to apply Bonne Bell cosmetics. The six-week course was taught by a former model and a fashion coordinator. The cost was $3.50 per course, which included a brown-and-white striped hatbox, and as many as six to eight classes were conducted each week. After a single radio spot, it wasn't necessary to advertise again for eight years.

Fred Lazarus Jr. forget the store's centennial? Not very likely, even though it was still thirty years in the future. *PC.*

Cheryl Galloway was about thirteen when she attended the self-improvement classes held in the annex. Upon completion of the program, she was asked if she'd like to model in the teen department. She readily agreed and continued to do so all the way through college, stopping only after she married. At a bridal show in the Assembly Center, Cheryl once worked with another young model named Barbara Bash, who later became the wife of professional golfer Jack Nicklaus.

On the eve of its anniversary, F&R Lazarus & Company had 278 members in the Twenty Year Club. To offset the relative reduction in sales associates, Lazarus installed bright red "U-Ask-It" intercoms throughout the store to provide immediate answers to customer questions. Now an associate was available at the push of a button.

The "Johnny Comes Marching Home, 1898" window display marking the end of the Spanish-American War. *CML.*

For six months before the centennial year, an intensive effort was made to improve merchandise selection, service and personnel planning throughout the store. Twenty historical dioramas were constructed, each one highlighting a significant event from local history, such as "Swedish Nightingale" Jenny Lind's 1851 concert, the dedication of Ohio Stadium in 1922 or the four "Immortal Chaplains" who gave up their life jackets when the USAT *Dorchester* sank during World War II.[19]

In September 1950, *Look to Lazarus*, a half-hour television show, debuted on WBNS-TV. Hosted by Pat Gleba (wife of local television personality Tom Gleba), it featured many of the VIP visitors to the store, with a special emphasis on noted clothing designers. The program was finally discontinued in 1952, having served its purpose.

The highlight of the first day of the centennial celebration was the grand opening of the newly remodeled "Third Floor of Fashions." Twenty-five models wore costumes illustrating the evolution of clothing design during the past century, while Lowell Riley provided a recital on a Wurlitzer organ hauled up to the Wedgewood Room. Meanwhile, Joe Weisberg entertained on the piano in the Collegienne Shop. Flower girls in colorful peasant costumes greeted customers with floral boutonnières.

Singer Patricia Wilson and pianist Dick Greenwald of WBNS-TV wrote and performed a series of in-store skits, emceed by Chet Long. For

Future Broadway star Patricia Wilson (shown with Roger Garrett) provided entertainment for the centennial in 1951. *PW.*

menswear, Pat sang, "Sam, You Made the Pants Too Long," and for the shoe department, "Put Your Shoes On, Lucy." Just eight years later, Pat costarred with Tom Bosley in the hit Broadway musical *Fiorello!*

Other events included the Centennial Showcase stage show at the Ohio Theatre, which featured associates singing, dancing and performing comedy routines. The 100th Anniversary Sale included a men's style show with Columbus press personalities and a guest appearance by radio and TV star Ed Sullivan (who also stuck around for the year's Eighty Year Old Party). Movie star Gloria Swanson added a bit of Hollywood glamour to the occasion.

In the midst of the yearlong observance, columnist Sylvia Porter of the *New York Post* used the term "boom" to describe the increased birth rate following the war. "Take the 3,548,000 babies born in 1950," she wrote. "Bundle them into a batch, bounce them all over the bountiful land that is America. What do you get? Boom. The biggest, boomiest boomy boom ever known in history." The so-called baby boom would drive merchandising for the next thirty years.

As always, the store continued to change and evolve. During the early 1950s, the men's and women's alteration rooms were "mechanized" (at Fred Jr.'s urging, no doubt). The first, third, fourth and fifth floors were redesigned to provide space for even more stock. The first complete sports apparel shop for men was added, reflecting the growing importance of leisure-time activities.

Even as Don Casto was refining the concept of the shopping center, the Lazarus family continued to resist the idea. According to Bob Lazarus Jr., who had returned to Columbus fresh out of college in 1950, they were "rebuilding our downtown building because after considerable discussion we decided we weren't going to build any branches."[20]

The suburban market consisted mainly of blue-collar workers. Since they couldn't provide as large an assortment of merchandise in a smaller branch, Lazarus management felt that they wouldn't be able to satisfy their customers and give them the kind of service they expected. So instead they decided to build a 350,000-square-feet addition onto the front of the store in 1952.

"We figured we'd build this, it could last another ten or fifteen years," Mr. Charles said, "and then we'd play around with branches and branch organizations."

Studies had suggested that the largest branch store that could be supported by the current population would be fifty thousand square feet. However, they also suspected that the addition would someday prove to be a burden on the main store and designed it so that it could be split off with the addition of elevators. This expansion was, Charles later admitted, "unfortunate."

Nevertheless, they continued to tweak the store's layout. The fifth floor was redone to accommodate increased stocks of decorative home furnishings, stamps, books and needlecrafts, while the fourth floor was redone for increased stocks of furniture, draperies and floor coverings. The Annex Lower Level, formerly a stock room, work center and delivery area, was converted to a selling floor. Sporting goods, luggage and cameras were moved from the Front Street Level North to the annex. Over the next couple of years, new garages were constructed at the Rich and Front Street corners.

During the 1950s, most families still had only one car, which the husband usually drove to work. Housewives and mothers (or even working women) often had no choice but to rely on the bus system or taxis when they wanted to go downtown to shop. With this in mind, Lazarus executives did whatever they could to make their store as inviting for female shoppers as possible. (Whenever they spoke of a shopper, it was almost always a "she.")

On March 14, 1955, the new Front Street Level Music Store opened with a live performance by the Lazarus Hot Jazz Combo. The legendary Al

A bird's-eye view of the Lazarus store, annex, parking garages and Auto Service Center. *CML.*

"Rags" Anderson, who had taught drums, xylophone and vibraphone at the store since 1939, was behind the drum kit. Charlie Cesner was on organ, Lee Knoll on guitar and Joe Weisberg on piano. Meanwhile, the Twenty Year Club had grown to 350 members.

Cynthia Robins, beauty editor of the *San Francisco Chronicle* and author of *The Beauty Workbook: A Commonsense Approach to Skin Care, Makeup, Hair, and Nails* (2001), began her love affair with cosmetics as a Lazarus associate. "I spent the summer between high school graduation and freshman year of college earning pin money by working as a temporary sales clerk," she recalled. "Assigned to the cosmetics department, I would rove from counter to counter, selling Elizabeth Arden makeup one day and expensive perfumes the next."

It wasn't long before Cynthia became a model for one of Revlon's makeup artists whose job was to attract customers by offering free makeovers. "I believe you're either born with the makeup gene or you're not," she said. "You either love cosmetics or you don't. Either you wear red lipstick, or it wears you."

Store hours changed once again in 1958, with both Mondays and Thursdays expanding from 12:30 p.m.–9:00 p.m to 9:30 a.m.–9:00 p.m. A year later, musical instruments were moved up to the fifth floor to allow more space for console stereos on the Front Street Level North. As walk/don't walk signs were springing up around the city, consideration was given

This 1958 jersey shirtdress ad was typical of its day. *PC.*

to permitting diagonal crossing at the Town and High intersection due to the hordes of pedestrians, especially during Remnant Days.

Public relations director Trent Sickles worked closely with city officials to improve the flow of traffic downtown. Lazarus had already loaned staff to assist city planners in laying out the innerbelt and outerbelt systems that continue to provide the parameters for transportation in Columbus. Their goal was to ensure that the downtown store would remain reachable within twenty-five minutes or less from any point in the surrounding metropolitan area.

Mr. Charles ("Chuck" to his friends and family) had spent four years building air bases during World War II. When he returned to Lazarus, he rapidly rose through the ranks, becoming executive vice-president in 1950 and then president in 1959. Although less personable than Uncle Bob, he likewise was in the habit of walking through the store each day. A time-honored tradition at Lazarus, it would later be called "Management By Walking Around" when it surfaced at Hewlitt-Packard in the 1970s.

While Leonard Deloia acknowledged that some people were afraid of the "serious-minded" Mr. Charles, he insisted that Charles had a rather dry sense of humor. For example, once when they were flying through a storm in a small airplane and were being tossed about by the turbulence, Charles asked Leonard, a devout Roman Catholic, if he "carried a rosary" with him. He was joking, of course, just to break the tension.

During the late 1950s, Mr. Charles helped found an organization called the 32 Group in an effort to improve race relations, noting, "We asked the black community to select sixteen representatives of the white community in whom they had faith. And, then, we asked them to choose sixteen representatives from the black community. We had no public meetings. We met behind closed doors. And, we met sometimes for days on end to listen to the complaints of the black community and to try to help them solve them."

Of all the sales associates who ever worked at Lazarus, none is more legendary than Joe Birkhead. Joe could sell anyone anything. Once a woman came to Lazarus to buy a suit for her husband to be buried in, and Joe sold her one—with two pairs of pants! On another occasion, Joe was overloaded with plastic ponchos, so he persuaded the wife of a dairy farmer to buy them to protect their cows from the rain. He even sold a coworker a double-breasted suit long after they had gone out of style.

On the other hand, Lazarus associates often went beyond the call of duty to provide service after the sale. Tom Stimmel's son recalls how his father, a longtime buyer for the store, spent many a Christmas Eve making the rounds to customers' homes to set up the toy train sets they had purchased. Bulk deliverymen regularly wrestled new hide-a-beds up three flights of narrow apartment building stairs and old ones back down again to dispose of them.

Lazarus employees were a cross-section of the community. In 1957, eighteen-year-old German immigrant Bruno Koehne stepped off the boat in America with two suitcases, a guitar and three English phrases: "Yes, sir," "No, sir" and "Thank you, sir." Sponsored by a relative in Columbus, he set about expanding his vocabulary by watching TV and reading comic books. Not long afterward, he took a bus downtown to Lazarus and, in broken English, asked for a job. He was promptly hired as a freight elevator operator. Just six months later, he had learned enough English to become an electrician's apprentice.

The same year, Zippy the Chimp, who had shot to fame as Dave Garroway "co-host" on NBC's *Today Show*, entertained a capacity crowd at the Lazarus Assembly Center. Other nonhuman celebrities to grace the store with their presence were Elsie, the Borden Dairy cow; TV star Lassie; and, some associates would argue, talk show perennial Zsa Zsa Gabor, who wanted them to replace the carpet and draperies in her room at the Neil House.

Bob Greene was eleven years old when he and a buddy, Kenny Stone, hopped a bus in Bexley to go downtown to Lazarus to see rockabilly star Dale Hawkins. As Greene, later a bestselling author, wrote, "[Hawkins] wasn't there for a full-scale concert; he and a rhythm-and-blues singer named Tommy Edwards, who had a smash hit with a song called 'It's All in the Game' that autumn, were coming to the F&R Lazarus department store…to autograph copies of their 45 rpm releases. For Hawkins, the current record was 'La-Do-Dada.'"[21]

In 1957, six-year-old Zippy
the Chimp entertained
a capacity crowd at the
Assembly Center. *CCJ.*

During 1959, Lazarus undertook the first major expansion of the store
since the 1920s. The façade was upgraded to signify that Lazarus "was a
modern retailer, changing with the times and capable of meeting the needs
of the new suburban shoppers," as Jonathan Schwartz wrote. Included in the
350,000-square-feet expansion were a pet supply shop, a hearing aid center, a
pantry and a bakery.

As early as the mid-1950s, Charles Lazarus and hundreds of associates
had participated in study programs on computers sponsored by AMC
(Associated Merchandising Corporation). They had tested experimental
programs developed for the Cleveland-based Bizmak computer. Finally, in
1960, an NCR 304 computer was installed at the main store to handle initial
sales reporting and accounts receivable.

The Collegienne Shops were renamed Junior Circle in 1960, and the
High Street addition was completed, the first major expansion since 1921,
providing an additional 350,000 square feet. The buildings were connected

by a bridge over Chapel Street. The entire downtown store was, once again, substantially redesigned and a new air-conditioning system installed. A year later, a fourth parking garage was built adjacent to the annex, providing space for six hundred cars, and an extra deck was added to Garage No. 3 at Rich and Front Streets.

"Boutiques" were all the rage in the 1960s, due to the splintering of the fashion market into "different approaches to wardrobe use and home decoration." At the same time, there was accelerated development of the store's service departments: shop-at-home services for carpets, upholstery, draperies, slipcovers and carpet, as well as a furniture cleaning service. There was also an increased emphasis on repair departments, from storm windows and home modernization to auto supply and installation services.

The annual baby animal exhibit appealed to kids of all ages, much as the live alligator had done years earlier. *PC.*

The store played host to a wide range of annual events in its sixth floor Assembly Center, from Girl Scout, Camp Fire Girl and Rainbow Girls conferences to flower shows and the popular baby animal farm each spring (where city kids could see baby chicks hatched). The Girl Scout Jamboree had once drawn as many as ten thousand girls. Most of these events had been discontinued by 1970.

For a young Rainbow Girl from Beavercreek, one of her fondest memories was attending the Grand Assembly in Columbus. "Imagine growing up on a farm then going to the home of the Ohio State Buckeyes—the thrill of seeing the capitol and all the buildings and stores," Marilyn Shumaker Gerkin recalled. "What young girl didn't love to go to Lazarus, look around at the clothing racks and take an armload of items to the dressing room? Trying on the clothes made you feel like a princess."

The girls may also have marveled at the "Wall of Air," an "invisible" doorway that used special fans to create an air cushion barrier separating the internal and external temperature differentials. Copied from a French store, it replaced the High Street door in 1960 and quickly became a tourist attraction. A member of the Levy family who owned the Union directly across the street purportedly joked, "They already have half the customers in central Ohio. Now, they're trying to suck the rest of them in."

The store was always quick to see the promotional potential of any unexpected happening. Photographer Herb "Topy" Topolosky related how he once received a call at his studio. "Herb, get over here quick," someone said. "We got a picture that has to be taken." So he walked over to Lazarus and found that they had a beautiful cat they were feeding milk. "This cat just took a six-month, six-week tour," he was told. Somehow it had crawled into a package the store had shipped off to a distant customer.

By 1961, Lazarus was selling just under $45 million worth of clothing annually (or six times more than its closest competitor). Some 40 percent of its customers were drawn from outside Columbus, reaching down as far as the Ohio River. According to *Forbes* magazine, no other department store in America so dominated its selling area.

For many years, Lazarus was the largest lineage and rotogravure (color) advertiser in the country. Because he managed the store's advertising budget, many people felt that Leonard Daloia also "controlled" the *Columbus Dispatch* and could ensure that a daughter's photo was published in the society section. His response to such requests was always the same: "The big 'L' on the roof [an illuminated "L" on the water tower] doesn't mean 'Leonard.'"

Look to Lazarus

After leasing Veteran's Memorial, John Kenley began staging his own versions of Broadway shows in Columbus, using popular stars from stage, screen and television—much like Broadway seems to be doing fifty years later. Gordon and Sheila MacRae opened the 1961 season in the musical *Bells Are Ringing* and were the first of many Kenley Players to meet and greet the public at the Lazarus Assembly Center.

Among the many other celebrities who made in-store appearances were movie stars Ann Miller, Cesar Romero, William "Hopalong Cassidy" Boyd and Polly Bergen; columnist Abigail "Dear Abby" Van Buren; Mouseketeer Jimmy Dodd; several Miss Americas; singer Jack Jones; athletes Arthur Ashe, Willie Stargell, Pete Rose and Jack Tatum; coach Woody Hayes; and talking, walking and dancing Barbie and Ken doll puppets. In 1982, Jim Palmer, star pitcher for the Baltimore Orioles, made an in-store appearance to sign copies of his Jockey brand underwear poster for a throng of his (mostly) female fans.

Not all Lazarus customers paid for their merchandise. Shoplifting was a persistent problem, so the company employed store detectives. Harry Seltzer, for one, looked the part. He was always skulking about, hiding behind columns and hoping to catch a thief in the act. Once he spotted a woman on the Front Street Level by the musical instruments and sporting goods departments dropping golf balls into the pockets of her skirt. When he confronted her about stealing the golf balls, she became irate and began jumping up and down. Suddenly, she "passed gas," emitting a bugle-like blast. Harry simply told her, "You can put that horn back, too."

The son of a local Lutheran minister once worked briefly as a store detective. One day, he was summoned to the first floor, told that there was a suspicious-looking man roaming the aisles and given a description. Sneaking up on the suspect, he was startled to find that the man was his father. He had been set up by his supervisor, who recognized the young man's father when he entered the store.

For thirty-two years, Tom Eviston worked as a buyer at Lazarus, starting just after the Korean War and ending when the store's headquarters moved to Cincinnati in 1986. He never had more fun than when he opened the Gourmet Food & Wine Shop in the annex. (When he was later reassigned to women's hosiery, one wag joked, "Tom's gone from hams to gams.")

Tom particularly enjoyed putting together the shop's special events, working with the trade commission of various foreign countries. For example, there were "festivals" built around the foods of France, Ireland, German, Italy and even some states such as Hawaii. Visits by politicians and

Tom Eviston had fun staging a Hawaiian luau at the Gourmet Food & Wine Shop as a way of involving the customers. *TE.*

celebrities were often part of the celebration, which might kick off with a wine tasting at the Columbus Museum of Art.

One year, Tom and his associates purchased a one-thousand-pound wheel of Wisconsin cheese and sold every piece in just half a day. The following year, they bought a two-thousand-pound wheel and sold it in a single day. Since they had to place their order a year in advance, they promptly upped it to a three-thousand-pound wheel for the next year and ran ads announcing, "The Big Cheese is Coming!"

When the one-and-a-half-ton wheel of cheese finally arrived, they had to roll it on dollies from the elevator across the sales floor. What they didn't anticipate was that the weight of the cheese would buckle the floor tiles, all of which had to be replaced. At this point, Charles Lazarus stepped in and forbade them to order anything larger.

Chapter 10
Lazabaloo

All business models have limited life spans. The Pony Express was a great success…for eighteen months. Two days after the transcontinental telegraph was completed, the Pony Express ceased operation.

Keuffel & Esser began manufacturing slide rules in the late 1800s. But when the pocket calculator was introduced in 1974, "slipsticks" became obsolete virtually overnight. Within a few months, K&E had shutdown production.

It's a long way from grinding stones to Post-It notes, but 3M (Minnesota Mining & Manufacturing) Company became a multinational corporation by emphasizing the "how" (innovation) rather than the "what" (product). If it had stuck with its original plan, the company would likely have gone bust long ago.

Lazarus had survived for more than a century by adapting to the times. But even as it evolved from a seller of "gent's furnishings" to a full-line department store, its core values remained the same. The touchstone for every decision the family made had always been that "the customer is always right." On one question, however, they most definitely felt that the customer was wrong: branch stores.

In 1960, Charles Lazarus explained their position:

> *Never a day goes by but some customer asks some executive of the store why we don't put a branch in her town. All of them seem to think it would be Utopia itself to have a handy Lazarus store. We believe that a branch Lazarus store would be a disappointment to customers. Lazarus means very broad assortments and store excitement to customers—you can't pack our kind of assortment and our kind of excitement into a small store. It takes 57 acres and 3,500 associates to put on our kind of show.*

Local photographer Julius Fortis Jr. captured this candid shot of a Lazarus shopper. *MLK.*

Although the family sincerely believed that they shouldn't do it, just two years later they finally succumbed to the inevitable and began opening stores in the suburbs. By the time Mr. Charles retired as chairman and CEO in 1981, the chain had grown to sixteen stores in three states. And he still didn't think much of the idea.

In the late 1940s, F&R Lazarus & Company had begun purchasing tracts of land in Lima, Newark and Marion while contemplating future growth. However, the first branch store would not be constructed until more than twenty years later, and it wasn't in any of those three communities. It was just six miles away.

The one-floor, free-standing store at West Broad Street and Phillipi Road on the western edge of Columbus was, admittedly, an experiment. It wasn't "where we wanted to go," Mr. Charles would later say, but they needed to find out if the organization could support two stores both from a management and a financial standpoint.

At eighty thousand square feet, Westland was one-sixteenth the size of the main store. Intended to serve customers within a ten-minute driving radius, it had space for 1,200 cars and was open until 9:00 p.m. on Saturdays and Sundays. It would soon have an automotive center as well.

Lazarus Westland did considerably better than anticipated. In the first three and a half months alone, it generated more than $3 million in revenue. Better yet, business at the main store increased 2.9 percent over the same period. That was a key point—its success was not due to a simple redistribution of sales from the downtown store.

Expanded to two floors in 1965 and enlarged again to 213,481 square feet in 1974, the Lazarus branch became the original anchor store for Westland

Shopping Mall. It also helped the company to reach another milestone: a $1 million sales day.

It would be easy to say that the Lazarus family had been mistaken, at least in the short run. True, the store was smaller, the selection less and the bells and whistles fewer, but most of their customers were not disappointed. The branch store met their needs. In the long run, though, the family couldn't have been more correct about what this development would portend.

The Westland store would eventually be rebranded Lazarus-Macy's in 2003's "Project Hyphen." Two years after that, it became simply Macy's in "Project Star" before finally closing forever in 2007. The experiment had lasted forty-five years, a more than respectable run. But some still maintain that it was the first nail in the coffin of F&R Lazarus & Company.

While Lazarus probably would have preferred to roll out additional branches at a more leisurely pace, its hand was forced when Sears Roebuck & Company purchased three large parcels of land on the north, east and west sides of Columbus for the purpose of constructing its own shopping malls. Unable to ignore this challenge on its doorstep, company officials approached the Chicago-based retailing giant about joining forces. Instead of being competitors, they would develop the properties together, sharing the costs and benefits. It was simply a matter of protecting market share.

Northland Mall, located at Morse and Karl Roads on the city's far north side, was their first joint venture, with Lazarus anchoring the west end and Sears the east of the open-air plaza. Halfway in between, shoppers could "meet under the clock tower," the mall's most notable feature. Opening in the spring of 1964 to record crowds, Lazarus Northland offered a three-level, 185,000-square-feet store with a separate 9,000-square-feet auto center.

About one-sixth the size of the downtown store, Lazarus Northland was, nevertheless, considered a full-line store department store. It housed fashions for men, women and children; a home furnishing and decorating center; major appliances, hardware and other staples; check cashing; bridal registry; a layaway plan; a coffee shop; a restaurant; and parking for five thousand.

Expanded in 1968 and again in 1974 to a total of 228,000 square feet, the Northland store was also deemed a success, although Lazarus management knew that sales were not keeping pace with expenses. A critical index—sales per square foot—was declining; they were spending more to earn less. The store finally closed in 2001 after thirty-seven years and was converted into offices for the Ohio Department of Taxation. The mall's end was no doubt hastened by the perception that it had become a magnet for unruly gangs of youth.

Bulk Storage Building No. 2 on West Whittier Street was also opened in 1964, the same year as Lazarus Northland. It was a companion to the original, highly acclaimed warehouse built fifteen years earlier. At 200,512 square feet, it was designed to facilitate the efficient handling of large quantities of merchandise. It also housed the store's package and bulk delivery fleet, as well as its carpeting installation crews. Both of these buildings were demolished in 2008, and the area was redeveloped into the Scioto Audubon Metro Park.

In 1963, the term "youthquake" was coined by Diana Vreeland, editor-in-chief of *Vogue*, to describe teenage domination of fashion, music and culture. Centered in London, this movement was responsible for everything from miniskirts to jumpsuits. The era's icons included such fashion models as Twiggy and Edie Sedgwick, designers Mary Quant and Betsey Johnson and artists Andy Warhol and Roy Lichtenstein, the latter a one-time instructor at Ohio State. As it turned out, the youthquake also became a major factor in the mallification of America.

Lazarus fashion coordinator Marianne "Mimi" Tomlinson was determined to raise the city's fashion awareness. In one season alone, she staged sixty-five separate fashion events, traveling to towns throughout central Ohio. No doubt she was instrumental in the selection of Columbus as the site of the Twenty-second Annual Coty American Fashion Critics' Award Show in 1964. It was the first time "the Winnies" was ever staged outside New York City. A former model, Mimi became the first local news anchorwoman.

To generate some "buzz" about its teen fashion line, Lazarus began staging a "Lazabaloo," a combination fashion show and concert, in the mid-1960s at the downtown store. The name was a takeoff on *Hullabaloo*, a 1965–66 NBC TV program that showcased popular musical groups of the day. Among the local bands that performed at the Lazabaloo were the Cheerful Earful, the Gears, the Sanhedrin Move, the Dantes, the Rebounds, the Fifth Order and the King Bees.

Members of the Cheerful Earful (Charlie Bleak, Jeff D'Angelo, George Mackline, Ben Messana, Rick Wilson and Bob Stephenson) were Upper Arlington High School students when they got hired to record a jingle for Lazarus Junior Girl's Shoppe. It was set to the tune of "Tobacco Road," but with these special lyrics ("dum dum" is the drum part):

(dum dum) G's for Girls
(dum dum) I's for In
(dum dum) R's for what's Really happenin'
L's for Lazarus

Among the bands that performed at the Lazabaloo (clockwise from right) were the Cheerful Earful, the Gears and the Fifth Order. *RS.*

The place to go
Where junior girls get their stylish clo-wo-wo-othes…

Although they received only fifty dollars (split six ways), it was great publicity for band. The song was heard for several years on local radio, as well as on the *In the Know* TV quiz show, which pits area high schools against one another for college scholarships.

Eastland, completed in 1967, was the city's first enclosed mall, with Lazarus anchoring the east end and Sears the west (and a two-story "rain lamp" sculpture in between dripping mineral oil). The 185,000-square-feet building was reconfigured in 1971 when the 73,000-square-feet Lazarus Home Store East debuted in a nearby strip mall. This outlet was devoted to furniture room settings and other big-ticket home goods.

According to Sue Robenalt, Home Store East earned a high return on investment, and Lazarus wanted to replicate the concept, but then the "Campeau thing" happened (the hostile takeover of Federated Department Stores).

In 1975, the Eastland store was expanded to 253,808 square feet. Both were rebranded Lazarus-Macy's in 2003 and Macy's in 2005 before closing a year later. Although Eastland Mall also had problems with gangs of unruly youth, it endeavored to address them by establishing written standards of conduct. However, the Association of Community Organizers for Reform Now (ACORN) promptly accused Eastland of "racial profiling."

The rise of the discount chains was a troubling development for traditional department stores such as Lazarus. To begin with, they were not even thought to be legal due to various fair trade laws prohibiting merchants from selling items below the manufacturer's suggested retail price. In addition, they deemphasized service both before and after the sale. Still, widespread acceptance by shoppers and suppliers eventually overcame these initial reservations.

Lazarus was the first Federated store to venture into the discount arena with the creation of Gold Circle Stores. Founded in Columbus in 1967, Gold

The Harmonaires were a popular Columbus vocal group that sometimes entertained at LAA events. *TE.*

Circle soon had outlets throughout Ohio, New York, Kentucky and western Pennsylvania. In 1984, it became the first major discounter to implement UPC barcode scanning (technology developed nearly twenty years earlier by Columbus-based Battelle Memorial Institute).

Among the discount chains, Gold Circle earned a reputation for being a cut above the rest. However, as Lazarus associate Dan Johnson learned when he transferred to a Gold Circle outlet near his home, the prices weren't the only thing discounted. His hourly wage of $1.60 was reduced by a nickel.

The discounter's fame apparently did not extend to members of the legendary New York Rock band the Velvet Underground. Once while performing in Columbus, they pulled into the parking lot of the Bistro, a nearby nightclub, and Maureen Tucker, the group's drummer, asked a bystander if Gold Circle was a bowling alley. She was disappointed to learn that it was not.

In 1986, Gold Circle merged with Richway, Federated's Atlanta-based chain of discount stores, in an attempt to compete with Dayton-Hudson's Target division. At the time, Gold Circle had fifty stores throughout the Midwest, while Richway owned thirty-one stores in the southern and southeastern states. The Gold Circle name was retained, and the chain continued to be based in Columbus. However, after Federated was acquired by Campeau Corporation in 1988, Gold Circle was broken up and sold off piecemeal.

The '60s were turbulent times, marked by the assassinations of President John F. Kennedy, Reverend Martin Luther King and Senator Robert F. Kennedy, as well as numerous racial disturbances and antiwar demonstrations across the nation. As 70 million baby boomers moved into adolescence and young adulthood, they began questioning and casting off the values of their parents' generation. Although Columbus remained an island of (relative) tranquility in a sea of unrest, it was not totally immune to these events.

Alarmed by high unemployment among inner city blacks, Charles Lazarus cautioned in 1968:

> *We are truly living on a volcano. To put it bluntly, a riot brings business to a shuddering halt. Customers stay home. Buses don't run. Employees can't get to work. Our plant is endangered. Police costs mount. Taxes go up. The impact of riots on balance sheets can be enormous. Am I justified in helping Columbus do those things that will improve the climate for business? I think I am.*

Believing that the continued prosperity of the city and the store were inextricably linked, Lazarus management worked diligently behind the scenes to address social issues. For example, Lazarus was one of the first merchants in the country to investigate the employment practices of its suppliers to ensure that they were not engaging in racial discrimination. However, in the scheme of things, the tea for eighty-year-olds was no longer felt to be a good use of store resources and was quietly discontinued.

In 1969, Mr. Charles moved up to chairman of Lazarus, and his good friend William Giovanello was tapped as the first non-family member to run the company in its nearly 120-year history. The same year, the Mansfield suburb of Ontario became home to the first Lazarus branch located outside the Columbus area when a 180,000-square-feet store opened at Richland Mall. Its distinctive "high hat" entrance tower quickly became a local landmark.

Expanded to 205,000 square feet in 1977, the Richland Lazarus was the first store in the chain to transmit sales from the cash register to a computer. As with many other branches, it was rebranded Lazarus-Macy's and then Macy's. When the original anchor store closed the next year, Macy's moved into the building previously occupied by Kaufmann's. It has seen service as a Halloween attraction, "The Undead Haunted Experience."

A Lazarus branch at the Kingsdale Shopping Center in Upper Arlington was launched in 1970, built of blue glazed bricks designed by Raymond Loewy, famed industrial designer. Initially, an 85,000-square-feet store specializing in fashion, it was enlarged to 105,302 square feet seven years later. This store pioneered the use of an inventory reconciliation system for its semiannual inventory. The Kingsdale store also experienced the Lazarus-Macy's dual-branding in 2003 before becoming Macy's in 2005.

Sue Robenalt became operations manager at Kingsdale after turning down the opportunity to manage stores in Newark, Lancaster and Zanesville. During her tenure, a young woman from Pakistan was employed at the store. For reasons that were never quite clear, the woman started a fire in a container. Although pregnant with her second child, Sue was the last person to evacuate the building ("I wasn't going to leave anyone behind!"). When the woman was subsequently brought to Sue's office, she offered no explanation for her actions but rather said simply, "I'm sorry. I hope I didn't hurt your baby."

In 1971, more than twenty years after the family considered moving into the Lima market, Lazarus opened a store in an established shopping center, Lima Mall. Developed by Edward J. DeBartolo Sr. of Youngstown, Lima Mall represented one of his first two ventures into larger, regional-class shopping malls.

Located in the suburban community of Elida, Lima Mall was initially 166,000 square feet and was later enlarged to 191,000 square feet in 1978. The Lazarus store featured the same "high hat" architecture first employed at Richland Mall.

This branch continued as Lazarus-Macy's in 2003 and as Macy's since 2005.

A year after President Richard Nixon instituted wage and prices controls in 1972, the first Indiana Lazarus store opened in the brand-new Castleton Square Shopping Mall in Indianapolis. This was a complete department store, including a Home Store and warehouse, and was outfitted with online Regitel cash registers. It was subsequently rebranded Lazarus-Macy's/Macy's. A second Indiana store followed in 1974 at Lafayette Square, a long-established Indianapolis shopping mall. In 1987, it was replaced by the rival William H. Block Company and has since been converted to a church.

A "Sportswear Week" ad from 1978 drawn by in-house artist Karen Ross-Ohlinger. *KRO.*

Both the Castleton and Lafayette malls were built by Edward J. DeBartolo Sr. The DeBartolo Corporation would soon become the leading mall developer in the country. At the time of his death in 1994, he owned 10 percent of all mall space in the United States.

Not long after Earl Burden became police chief of Columbus, Charles Lazarus instructed Leonard Deloia to facilitate a meeting between Burden and Amos Lynch, publisher of the *Call & Post* ("Ohio's Black News Leader"). He felt that it would be a good idea if the two men could "get to know each other" over lunch in the executive dining room. Mr. Charles hoped to head off racial tensions by improving communications between law enforcement and the African American community. Naturally, he did not want any credit.

When Robert Lazarus Sr. died in 1973, the *Enthusiast* published a cartoon of "ARELF" with a tear running down his cheek. ARELF, an elf doll, was the mascot of the Twenty Year Club and for twenty-two years had been presented to Uncle Bob at each annual banquet, dressed up to reflect the event's theme.

Even after he retired in 1969 at the age of seventy-nine, he didn't stop working. At 9:30 a.m. on the morning after his retirement, he walked into the store, and an associate said, "Why Mr. Robert, I thought you retired yesterday."

"I did," he replied. "That's why I'm not here until now." Three months later, his younger brother, Fred Jr., died as well. The old order was passing.

"Most of us who started at Lazarus didn't think of making it a career," Sue Robenalt said. She started out working nights and weekends at Kingsdale as a cosmetics model, earning 8 percent commission. After she entered the management development program, she actually had to take a cut in pay to $9,500 per year. At the time, female associates were expected to wear three-piece suits and were sent home if they weren't appropriately attired.

Women's Wear Daily reported in 1974 that sales at branch stores exceeded $100 million, which was true. However, there was a downside. As Mr. Bob put it, "Multiple locations gets you more volume, but you transfer volume as well." Having three locations might triple expenses, but it did not triple sales. Sales at Westland had more than justified the investment, but that wasn't the case at Northland and Eastland.

Unlike many retailers that had separate buyers and sellers, Lazarus held its buyers accountable for the profitability of their

ARELF-1972

The Lazarus Enthusiast

FEBRUARY 9, 1973   VOLUME 60   NUMBER 6

It was a sad day when Robert Lazarus Sr. passed away, and even ARELF shed a tear. *TE.*

departments. They were expected to roam the sales floor daily to meet customers, answer questions and discuss the merchandise selection. This system could not survive the addition of branch stores. As Lola Hanson, a buyer for forty-three years, said, "You can only be so many places at one time; you're only one person."

"The larger the store gets," Fred Jr. said, "the further management are likely to get from the customers, and they begin to pay too much attention to techniques and much too little attention to the person who is really paying for their growth, their salaries and for everything else, which is the person that comes in to buy from them."

After a couple of years in college, Jerry Wayne Bowling had landed a job in window display at Morehouse Fashion. When he won a national contest sponsored by Burlington Fabrics, he crossed the street to take a similar position at Lazarus. He felt that it was a better opportunity because Lazarus was the premier department store in town; as a division of Federated, it would provide him with greater exposure in the industry.

Even though advertising and display were separate units within the Lazarus art department, the two staffs worked hand in hand. "One wonderful day," the head of advertising saw Jerry's photography portfolio and offered him the chance to do a fashion shoot for the store. Soon, his work was appearing in such national magazines as *Glamour*, *Mademoiselle* and *Town and Country*. Although he later took a job at the Limited, he credited Lazarus with giving him his big break.

Many aspiring artists "went to school" at Lazarus because the typical art school did not turn out the kinds of artists needed. Karen Ross-Ohlinger was one. Although she referred to herself as self-taught, she readily acknowledged that she "learned a great deal from the marvelous artists, copy writers, and art directors that I was privileged to work with" in the Lazarus art department.

There were actually two advertising departments, one for the budget merchandise and the other for everything else. Karen worked in "the one behind the china department on the fifth floor." They entered their work area by walking through the doors of the china stockroom and down a ramp.

The artists worked in ten-foot-square cubicles containing their drawing boards, shelves, a counter and "probably a radio." Karen and her coworkers listened to the television soap opera *All My Children* (which could be picked up on the radio) every afternoon at one o'clock while busily sketching, but they never actually saw it so she did not know what the actors looked like.

They often worked from live models using actual merchandise borrowed from the store. One day, according to Leonard Daloia, they noticed that some fur coats were missing. It turned out that a member of the night cleaning crew was dropping the furs out of the window to an accomplice, who would retrieve them. The art department windows were subsequently welded shut.

One valued piece of equipment was a lucidograph (nicknamed "Lucy"), a huge apparatus located in the hallway outside the art department. It was used to enlarge or reduce various items of merchandise they needed to draw. It was a very laborious process, and only one artist could use it as a time.

Gradually, computers made the "Lucy" obsolete even as the artists' roles were being redefined, reduced and eliminated. In the final days, the few remaining associates felt like children in a deserted playground. They would swing from the overhead hooks on the long idled conveyor system or tiptoe through abandoned offices where yellowing paperwork remained undisturbed on desks. They were explorers, searching the ruins of some great and ancient civilization and wondering what had caused its downfall.

Chapter 11

Like Night and Day

With overhead continuing to rise, Lazarus was forced to either increase prices or reduce expenses. In many businesses, the first impulse is to cut training, and Lazarus was no different. Management had come to recognize that a skilled sales force was of less importance because of strides made in product packaging. Increasingly, the merchandise sold itself. All the associate had to do was ring up the sale.

"The days when working at Lazarus represented the first, last and only job that many of its employees would ever have were gone," Jonathan Schwartz observed. Associates or not, less skilled employees did not require the same level of compensation. It may not have been how the Lazarus family preferred to do business, but they had few options.

Instead of a doorway to a career, a job at Lazarus was now just a job—good for gaining some initial work experience, building a resume or picking up extra income but, with rare exceptions, little else. Funds for anything else not directly related to selling were also slashed. Gone were the in-store demonstrations, puppet shows, book signings, baby animal farms and concerts. The circus had left town. Turnover of sales staff increased industry-wide.

In 1973, Lazarus Capri, a budget fashion and accessories store, opened in the aging Town & Country Shopping Center, replacing the former Boston Store. A modest 33,739 square feet in size, it was intended to recapture some of the market share that Lazarus was losing to discounters. Later, it moved to the former Union/Halle's building at Town & Country before closing in 1992.

During the next few years, two more Capri shops were set up in the former Tempo-Buckeye Mart buildings at Upper Arlington's Northwest Center (at the corner of Reed and Henderson Roads) and Westerville's Westerville

Square. Tempo-Buckeye Mart had grown out of the old Columbus-based Cussins & Fearn Company, founded in 1893. Both stores were closed in 2002 and 2004, respectively, after becoming Lazarus-Macy's hyphenates.

Sue Robenalt said that the concept behind Capri was "brand-name fashions at a reasonable price." When William Giovanello became president of Lazarus, Sue was assigned to manage the Capri store on Henderson Rd. and given his son, Joe, as a trainee. From time to time, Mr. Bill would "pop in to see how he was doing," always unannounced.

"By 1975, discounters and chain department stores of the Sears' and Penney's sort captured 89 percent of all 'department store' sales," Jan Whittaker noted. "What was known as a department store had radically changed since the 1920s, when few of these enterprises would have been perceived as department stores at all." While Lazarus had not lost sight of the original vision, it was changing, too.

A few feathers were ruffled when Lazarus published its first lingerie catalogue in 1976. "We got about 60 letters of complaint about the photographs," acknowledged Leonard Deloia, vice-president of promotions. "At the time, I guess, they were too sensuous for Columbus." Twenty years later, locally based Abercrombie & Fitch would push the envelope considerably further when its catalogue featured nude models in suggestive poses.

In 1978, the four-year-old Washington Square Mall in Indianapolis, another DeBartolo project, acquired a Lazarus store (it was closed in 2002). Meanwhile, the Twenty Year Club had increased to 1,112 members, while 4,009 associates participated in the Retirement Income and Thrift Incentive (RITI) program.

Musicians Dave Murphy and Pat Mogan were hired by Lazarus for St. Patrick's Day in 1979, to serve as strolling minstrels in the flagship store, singing and playing the Irish tunes they had previously performed only at meetings of the Shamrock Club. The two were so well received that they quickly put together a band, the Irish Brigade, which enjoyed enormous success over the next couple of decades and spawned the local Celtic music scene.

Under pressure from Federated, a fourth Indianapolis Lazarus store, Greenwood Park Mall (promoted as the favorite spot of "famous comedian" Daryll Bluett), was opened in 1980. It was followed by stores at Barboursville, West Virginia's Huntington Mall in 1981, and Evansville, Indiana's Eastland Mall in 1982. However, there was one problem: the Lazarus name meant nothing to potential customers in these regions. All of these stores were later rebranded Lazarus-Macy's/Macy's.

Mr. Charles had seen his worst fears come true—he no longer could devote his attention to the small details he felt were necessary to operate a successful business:

Like Night and Day

My father, then Uncle Bob, and I and Ralph used to stand at the side door at Christmas every night and wish everyone a Merry Christmas and a Happy New Year. We couldn't do that anymore. As new stores opened, I tried to get out two or three days before Christmas to all the stores to wish people a Merry Christmas and a Happy New Year and thank them for all they'd done. And finally, I had to go around by helicopter. Which I did. I took off from the roof of the stores or parking lots. But those personal touches aren't here anymore.

"By the early 1980s, downtowns could be divided into those that still had at least one major department store—such as Kaufmann's in Pittsburgh, Lazarus in Columbus, and Mier and Frank in Portland—and those that did not," according to Larry Ford in *America's New Downtowns: Revitalization or Reinvention?* "In the former, downtown remained at least a minor shopping destination, while in the latter retailing all but disappeared."

The "echo boomers," children of postwar baby boomers, began arriving in the late 1970s. Also known as "Generation X," there are 80 million or more of them, and they are having a tremendous impact on all segments of the economy, especially as their parents' generation "grays." Their hallmark is diversity. They have high expectations, seek immediate gratification and are voracious consumers. Many of the products they buy weren't even dreamed of a generation ago and will become obsolete even quicker. By 1980, there were twenty-two thousand shopping centers and malls nationwide, and these were the playgrounds where they had grown up.

The retirement of Mr. Charles as chairman in 1981 may have been the tipping point in the store's history. He was the fourth and final generation of Lazarus men to head the company. His replacement, Michael J. Boyle, came from Bamberger's and the Melville Corporation. (Just a year later, Ralph Lazarus retired as chairman of Federated, and his replacement was not a family member, either.)

"Without a Lazarus walking around and checking on things," Lola Hasson said, "the difference was like night and day." Boyle came from the New York/New Jersey area, had no connection to Columbus and harbored no innate affection for the community. The lavish New Year's Eve parties for associates had already fallen by the wayside, a sacrifice to the new reality of doing business.

In 1982, Shillito's and Rike's of Dayton merged with Federated Department Stores. Four years later, the seventeen Lazarus stores were combined with the fourteen Shillito-Rike's, and the headquarters was moved to Cincinnati (home of Federated Department Stores), resulting in a loss of nine hundred jobs in Columbus. All of the stores would now operate under the Lazarus name.

Mr. Bob, the only family member still involved with the store, learned of the move as he was leaving on an African safari with Columbus zoo director Jack Hanna. Although initial reports were that he was extremely angry about the decision, he later clarified that he "wasn't mad. Just very, very sad." He also said that if the family had still been in charge, "obviously, it would have been very different."

For a time, things continued pretty much as before. In the fall of 1983, "Inspiration Italy" was chosen as the theme of an Italian import fair. It was exactly the type of thing for which the Lazarus department store was known. However, such events would become increasingly rare.

When Buckeye quarterback Mike Tomczak wanted to give modeling a shot, Lazarus, long a supporter of Ohio State athletics, featured him in a full-page ad in the June 1983 issue of *Columbus Monthly*. Even though he donated his forty-dollar fee to charity and neither he nor the school was mentioned by name, Mike quickly found himself in hot water with the NCAA. He had violated a rule prohibiting athletes from appearing in advertisements and was declared ineligible to play. A month later, the Eligibility Committee reinstated him, persuaded that it was an innocent mistake.

In 1986, another Lazarus branch was opened at Indian Mound Mall in Heath, Ohio. The store was hyphenated Lazarus-Macy's in 2003 and then closed a year later. About the same time, a massive Lazarus rebranding program was initiated that affected many members of the Federated family.

All the Shillito-Rike's outlets were now converted into Lazarus stores. It may have been done more out of a desire to show Wall Street that Federated was "doing something" than as a result of some well-thought-out marketing strategy. Grumblings of an "identity crisis" at Federated Department Stores soon gave birth to rumors that real estate developer Al Taubman or retailing magnate Les Wexner was considering a takeover bid.

Shillito's Tri-County Mall store in Cincinnati, launched in 1960, underwent the full Shillito-Rike's to Lazarus-Macy's to Macy's metamorphosis. However, the Rike's stores in the Kettering Shopping Center (Kettering, Ohio, 1961) and Salem Mall (Trotwood, Ohio, 1966) did not, closing in 1998 not long after they were renamed Lazarus. A small Shillito's outlet that had opened in Oxford, Ohio, in about 1968 was completely rebranded before closing in 2004.

The Dayton Mall Rike's, unveiled in 1962, and the Beechmont Mall Shillito's and Western Woods Mall Shillito's, both opened in Cincinnati in 1982, all became Lazarus stores. The first two went through the Lazarus-Macy's/Macy's rebranding, while the third closed in 1997 after being scaled back from three to two floors. In 1999, a thirty-six-year-old man walked into the Dayton Mall Lazarus store and pointed two handguns at shoppers before killing himself.

Four Shillito's stores in Kentucky underwent the full rebranding: Louisville's Oxmoor Center (opened in 1970) and Jefferson Mall (1979), Lexington's Fayette Mall (1971) and Florence's Florence Mall (1977). Afterward, they continued on as Macy's stores.

The downtown Shillito's at Seventh and Race Streets was closed in 1997 under the Lazarus nameplate, while the Kenwood Mall outlet was converted to a Lazarus Furniture Galley in 1989. It replaced the Shillito's/Lazarus store that had moved across the street to the new Kenwood Towne Centre. Both later morphed into Lazarus-Macy's/Macy's.

Another significant change occurred in 1987 when operations at the store's two Bulk Service Buildings on Whittier Street, as well as at the main store, were moved to Sharonville, just outside Cincinnati. Sharonville was home to several trucking companies. At the same time, distribution centers in Indianapolis, Dayton and Cincinnati were also closed. In making the announcement, the senior vice-president of operations explained that a capacity analysis concluded that the company would be out of business by spring if it did not consolidate and modernize its operations.

Other, more subtle changes were taking place as well. The popular Lazarus Book and Author Luncheons, held three times a year, were discontinued after B. Dalton Bookseller took control of the downtown bookstore. Over the years, these events featured such people as children's author and illustrator Tasha Tudor, poet and memoirist Maya Angelou, football coach and owner Paul Brown and travel writer William Least Heat-Moon. Although Dalton's management held out the hope that they would resume, they didn't. In fact, the bookseller was soon bought out by Barnes & Noble.

Homeworks at Lazarus was a short-lived concept introduced in 1987 at a time when many major retailers were experimenting with store sizes. Having already opened fifty-thousand-square-feet specialty stores in Heath, Westerville, Upper Arlington and Whitehall, Lazarus debuted a twenty-thousand-square-feet Homeworks adjacent to the Henderson Road store and another in Indianapolis. This outlet carried moderately priced, contemporary, ready-to-assemble furniture. It was expected to appeal to first-time home buyers, apartment dwellers and cottage owners.

With the acquisition of twelve Indiana-based William H. Block's stores, Lazarus now had full-service stores in Columbus, Cincinnati, Dayton and Indianapolis, in addition to eight more stores in Indiana, two in Springfield and two in Grand Rapids, Michigan. The expectation was for Lazarus to exceed $1 billion in sales during 1987. It didn't.

When Lazarus set a goal of earning $1 billion in revenue, Sue Robenalt came up with the idea of creating a program to ensure that all managers were on the same page. They organized focus groups to develop ways to differentiate Lazarus from other retailers—to be "better than the best" (which, in their mind, was Nordstrom). This open exchange of ideas was one of the most rewarding experiences of her career. Then they eliminated her job.

The original eight-story Indianapolis Block's store—"the Pride of Hoosierdom"—had attracted seventy thousand customers in one day when it was opened in 1911. However, it was closed forever in 1993, six years after it was absorbed by Lazarus. As *Indianapolis Monthly* declared. "Hoosier pride isn't transferable."

As far as is known, the only wedding to ever take place in the store was on April 30, 1987, when Deborah Hamill, manager of the shoe department, married Kevin Cummings in the basement Events Center. The bride, her father and her mother were all longtime Lazarus employees, with a total of seventy-five years of service. Deborah had been introduced to her fiancé by a coworker.

Naturally, the cake, shoes, dress and flowers were all supplied by Lazarus, too. Because the store was open during the ceremony, some of the guests had to return to their stations immediately afterward to assist customers with sales. As Deborah quipped, "We don't want to detract anything from the register."

Encouraged by the success of the Heath store, which handled only apparel, cosmetics and accessories, Lazarus opened branches at Wesleyan Park Plaza (Owensboro, Kentucky), River Valley Mall (Lancaster, Ohio) and Colony Square Mall (Zanesville, Ohio). The first two were rebranded Lazarus-Macy's/Macy's before closing in 2006 and 2007, respectively. Colony Square was still called Lazarus when the lights were turned off in 2002.

"A new store is like a drug," former Lazarus chairman Mark A. Cohen told Adrienne Bosworth of *Columbus Monthly*. "Take the drug, feel the effect." It was easy, he admits, to ignore the old stores while building up new markets in Kentucky and West Virginia, where the "customers were gold waiting to be mined."

By the mid-'80s, the Federated motto had become "Expense the way to profit." Efforts to obtain corporate approval for renovations went nowhere. Salaries for sales staff were cut. The Lazarus stores were rapidly going to seed, and the customers did not fail to notice. Management at Lazarus came to refer to Federated executives as "seagulls" because they "flew in, ate your food, crapped all over you and flew away."

Chapter 12

Christmas on
Candy Cane Lane

For generations of Ohioans, Lazarus was as important in the development of their holiday traditions as the church, Charles Dickens or Coca-Cola (which popularized the modern image of Santa Claus wearing its corporate colors—red and white). It just wasn't Christmas without the annual family pilgrimage to the flagship store. Looking back over half a century, Barbara Robinson, author of *The Best Christmas Pageant Ever*, fondly recalled the magical bus rides she would take with her mother from her home in Portsmouth to shop at Lazarus.

"Black Friday," the day after Thanksgiving, marks the beginning of the holiday shopping season. That is the day when merchants learn whether they will be "in the black" (profitable) for the year. When President Abraham Lincoln first established Thanksgiving in 1863, however, it was intended as solemn occasion on which people were urged to reflect on the (mostly nonmaterial) blessings of the previous year.

Although it originally moved around a bit, by the beginning of the twentieth century Thanksgiving had been set as the last Thursday of November. That didn't satisfy Fred Lazarus Jr., though. In 1939, he persuaded President Franklin Roosevelt to move it to the fourth Thursday of November, thereby ensuring an extra week of Christmas shopping and boosting revenues. But Fred apparently neglected to tell his brother Simon. When he heard the news and realized its impact on the Buckeye football schedule, Uncle Si bellowed, "What damn fool got the president to do that?" Fred replied, "You're looking at him."

While everyone knew that Lazarus had the "real Santa," the department store Santa was an established institution well before the "Jolly Old Elf" took up residence in Columbus. In 1841, J.W. Parkinson of Philadelphia hired a man to dress up as Kriss Kringle and climb out of his store's chimney in order to spur sales. Forty years later, the Boston Store in Brockton, Massachusetts, took the idea one step further when it hired Edgar, a chubby, bearded Scottish immigrant with a hearty laugh, to play Santa Claus.

Dave Hundley was neither the first nor the last Lazarus Santa, but he was one of the best and still looks the part some thirty years later. One day, while he was helping out at his parents' tavern, a customer happened to mention that Lazarus was looking for Santas. Since Dave liked being around kids, he decided to look into it and was promptly hired for the downtown store.

The day after Thanksgiving 1979, Dave went through a crash course on how to be Santa Claus (the "real Santa," the instructor emphasized). Though it only paid minimum wage, to a young man in his early twenties it was enough. Besides, Dave quickly discovered that the job had some unexpected perks: children often brought Santa cookies and other goodies.

Everyone knew that the only "real Santa" was at Lazarus, even though the store actually had multiple Santas at any given time. *PC.*

Another chance encounter led to Dave's becoming Santa in print as well. He was taking a smoke break in the Highlander Grill when he suddenly found himself surrounded by a contingent from Lazarus's in-house advertising department. After looking him up and down, he was told that they wanted to use him as their Santa Claus model. For twenty dollars per hour, he wasn't about to turn them down. He was subsequently photographed for several full-page color advertisements in the *Columbus Dispatch*.

One of Dave's favorite memories is when Diane, a former girlfriend, brought her little brother to see Santa. She did not recognize Dave beneath the makeup, padding and fake beard and was astonished when Santa told her brother all about his parents, sister, dog, where they lived and so on. Both the ex-girlfriend and her younger brother were believers that day.

Dave Hundley was not the only "real Santa" at that time. He wasn't even the only one that night. A female assistant, or Santa Belle, would direct the children down one of three or four partitioned paths to separate "houses," each containing a Santa Claus. In 1987, there were nine Santas and sixty Santa Belles to contend with sixty thousand children or, as *Columbus Dispatch* columnist Mike Harden observed, the same number as marines who landed on Iwo Jima.

Mary Krieger remembers her mother dressing her and her four siblings in their Christmas outfits and lining them up for a picture at home before beginning the forty-five-minute drive from Hebron to visit Santa. "The real Santa always resided at the North Pole on the sixth floor at Downtown Lazarus," she said. "Everyone knew that!" As they approached the store,

WBNS radio deejay Irwin Johnson joined with Lazarus to promote Christmas seals in 1946. *PC.*

123

there were a few people out front begging for coins. Her father always gave them money, reminding his kids how lucky they were to have warm clothes, a nice home and parents who brought them to see Santa.

Just a year before, Harden's colleague, Jack Willey, had related an anecdote about a young couple who became engaged with Santa's help. While sharing Santa's lap, a less than comfortable situation for Santa, the young man said that what he wanted most for Christmas was to marry his girl. He then presented her with a ring. The readers never found out what her answer was, but it's a sure bet that no one who witnessed the scene ever forgot it.

Julie Secrest, former Delaware city council member, was a Santa Belle while working her way through Ohio State University in the late '50s. Lazarus fashion coordinator Marianne Tomlinson got her start providing costumes for the young women who functioned as Santa's helpers. Besides serving as kid wranglers, the Santa Belles also operated the express elevator to Santaland, led shoppers in singing Christmas carols and helped out in other ways. When it was time for Santa to take a break, a Santa Belle would inform the waiting children that "Santa needs to feed his reindeer."

Santaland received major renovation in 1989 when it was moved from the sixth floor to the East Basement, and the animatronic display ("Christmas Comes to Tudortown") was added. As they made their way to Santa's house, a family could view the moving tableaux and read the large scrolls, which told the story of a town populated by animals and their efforts to get Santa to remember them at Christmas. A similar presentation, "The Enchanted Village of Tudor Towne," can still be seen at the National Christmas Center in Paradise, Pennsylvania.

In 1992, Lazarus greatly scaled back its Santaland. For first time since 1912, the downtown location did not sell toys, although Mr. Tree, the Santa Belles and the holiday displays remained. Senior Vice-President Jerry Gafford assured shoppers that even though the toys were gone, "There's only one real Santa, and he's at Lazarus." Santa last visited Lazarus in 1994. The "real Santa" had been made redundant by an imposter in a red suit who had set up shop in the connecting City Center Mall.

For many years, Santa arrived at Lazarus at the conclusion of a holiday parade that began in Clintonville and came to end at the front door of the downtown store. TV and radio personality Gene Fullen played Santa a time or two, as did "Spook" Beckman and other local celebrities.

As a marshal in the Santa Claus parade, Tom Eviston patrolled High Street dressed as a pirate, unwittingly frightening one child. As Tom ran from the scene, he tripped, turned a complete cartwheel and managed to land on his feet, to the delight and applause of onlookers. Little did they realize that he had actually injured his back.

Herb Topy, official photographer for the parade, said that it was eventually discontinued in favor of having Santa make his grand entrance via a "whirlybird" (helicopter). Naturally, he went along, even though it was icy and snowing. They flew around the city, circling and waving at people who had assembled in schoolyards and stadiums, before landing at the downtown Lazarus garage. Afterward, one of the women coordinating the event told him, "You know, Herb, we had you insured just in case."

For many years, Lazarus sponsored a Santa Claus parade that began in Clintonville and proceeded south on High Street to the store. *CCJ.*

Santa wasn't the only celebrity to appear yearly in the parade. Bob "Flippo, the Clown" Marvin often rode a float. Luci Van Leeuwen, host of WBNS-TV show *Luci's Toyshop*, was joined by her puppet friends such as Stanley Mouse, Pierre and Lion (voiced by the station's versatile Chuck White during the show's 1960–72 run). Santa returned the favor by paying a yearly visit to *Luci's Toyshop*, where he would use her workshop to make toys and read children's letters sent by Luci's viewers. (According to Herb Topy, WBNS-TV's original Santa was comedian Jonathan Winters back in about 1950!)

Luci's show first introduced another Lazarus Christmas character, Mr. Tree, a large, semianimated puppet that talked and sang, voiced by Raymond Stawiarski (and others, including Dave Hundley). Mr. Tree could always be found in Santaland at Lazarus, delighting and, occasionally, terrifying children by speaking to them directly, answering questions and cracking jokes. The young men who voiced Mr. Tree in-store were told: 1) No off-color jokes or songs; 2) Remember: You are Santa's Christmas tree and friend; and 3) The trees at the other stores are your "branches." You are one hundred and *tree* years old.

The Ketcham brothers seem delighted by the annual Christmas train layout at Lazarus. *RK.*

There was much more to Lazarus Christmas than Santaland, the parade and Mr. Tree, of course. Holiday decorating and tree trimming had taken off after department stores started offering ornaments for sale, many imported from Germany, where Christmas markets dated back to 1434. Although Lazarus may not have been the first local store to promote Christmas (and other holidays), by World War I it had become the most prominent. A highlight for many adults and kids was the deluxe model train layout. There were also breakfasts with Santa (or, in the season, the Easter Bunny), with music provided by pianist Jane McDannold.

In 1966, the Lazarus Glee Club recorded a flexi-disc, *Christmas At Lazarus*, which included spoken messages from both Mr. Charles and Uncle Bob. It was not unusual to hear choral groups singing in the downtown store, particularly during holidays. Sometimes they were arranged on the escalator stairs to serenade customers when the store opened in the morning. Herb Yenser, longtime vocal music teacher at Upper Arlington High School, led choruses at both Lazarus and the *Columbus Dispatch* for many years.

For Christmas 1963, the fifty-thousand-gallon water tower on the roof of the Lazarus building was converted into a "Tree of Lights." Designed by Glenn Harrod and strung by electrician Harold Nichols, this display shone brightly two hundred feet above street level every year but two (the exceptions occurring during the energy crisis of the 1970s). It was finally discontinued in 1990 due to decreased visibility caused by modern construction. Another "tree" was created by cascading lights down the High Street façade. Altogether, the display incorporated five and a half miles of wire and ten thousand bulbs.

The first "Tree of Lights" was erected over the water tower for Christmas 1963. *CD*.

Lazarus was especially known for its holiday windows. The "big window" at Town and High Streets was always the highlight. An elevated ramp was built in front of it so that little children could get up close. Marianne Tomlinson recalled that Bob Morehead, head of the display department, would make "tiny cookies and tablecloths and little, bitty things." Among the many other people who made contributions to the window displays were local artists Gordon Keith and Ivan Pusecker.

Keith, of Gordon Keith Originals, is perhaps best remembered today for his creation of the State Auto Insurance Christmas Nativity Scene at 518 East Broad Street, which was originally erected annually on the steps of the Ohio Statehouse. Thousands of people still visit the life-sized tableaux, particularly on Christmas Eve, when the baby Jesus appears in the manger.

For Ivan "Lefty" Pusecker, the holiday windows were a family affair. His son, Nick, remembered working in the garage with his dad and brother to construct the figures for the windows. Ivan would begin with a drawing, turn that into a clay sculpture and then, with the help of his sons, cast the clay in plaster and use the resulting mold to fashion papier-mâché figures. Ivan's wife, Peg, made the costumes. As a family, the Puseckers would sit together

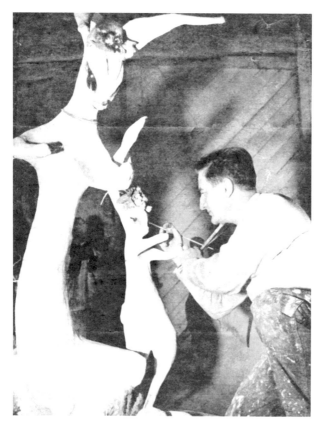

Above: Zeppelin mania was at a high point in 1930 when one of the rigid airships was incorporated into this Christmas display. *PC.*

Left: Ivan Pusecker oversaw the construction of papier-mâché figures based on his original sketches. *LPR.*

Right: During the late 1940s, Ivan Pusecker created numerous sketches for proposed Christmas display figures. *LPR.*

Below: Ivan Pusecker charged $57.50 for each of these six-foot-tall *Lady Deer* sculptures. *LPR.*

every week and pore through magazines looking for images to add to the ever increasing folio that their father used for inspiration.

Ivan got his start when he was asked to create a window display to celebrate the armistice in 1945. It was actually built in anticipation of the ceasefire so it would be ready to go as soon as the war ended. Although he designed and built displays for many holiday displays, including Easter, Christmas was always the most spectacular. In the Pusecker home, Christmas actually began more than six months earlier. The displays needed to be finished by the end of summer to make it into the stores on time.

In 1957, Lazarus introduced the "Secret Gift Shop," where children could buy Christmas presents in their own special store. Other than the Lazarus associates, no adults were permitted to enter the gift shop, which at first was simply an area set off by pipe and drapes with a doorway no more than forty-eight or fifty inches high. After the child made his or her purchase (perhaps a piece of costume jewelry for mom and a bottle of Old Spice for dad), it was placed in a hinged box so the child could look at it whenever he or she wanted.

In the late 1970s, Lorelei ("Lolly") Kerchner was a special events assistant working for longtime Lazarus associate Betty Raymond. Lolly got the

In 1957, Lazarus created the Secret Santa Gift Shop specifically for kids. *PC.*

idea of spreading a special type of holiday cheer to patients at Children's Hospital who had to stay in the hospital in the days preceding Christmas. She contacted the Child Life Department at Children's Hospital and proposed something called "Santa's Secret Village," where patients could "shop" for their parents and siblings from donated gifts.

F&R Lazarus & Company had a long-established relationship with Children's Hospital. Going back as far as 1915, Fred Jr., Simon, Bob Sr. and Bob Jr. had all served on the hospital's board. The Child Life Department liked Lolly's idea so much that it decided to promote it in the local media. The hospital's public relations director, Randy Ketcham, met with Lolly to create a major front-page story for the *Columbus Dispatch*. The two hit it off so well that in September 1980, Randy and Lolly were married.

Christmas at Lazarus was such a special occasion that many shoppers wished they could take it home with them. Starting in 1986, they could—sort of. When LazzieBear was first introduced, the plush, white teddy bear with the red hat and scarf was an instant sensation. A rumored 400,000 were sold in just four weeks as bear hysteria swept the state.

LazzieBear was still going strong in 1988 when he was incorporated into the Santaland display. *PC.*

Available for ten dollars with a thirty-five-dollar purchase, LazzieBear soon had competition from Kmart's Christmas Bear, Meijer's Polar Pal, Big Bear's Honey Jo Bear and J.C. Penney's Bumble Bear. LazzieBear was used in ads and on signs and merchandise such as glass mugs, shirts, candles and snow globes. Kids could even meet LazzieBear "in person" in Santaland.

LazzieBear was so popular that he got his own "watchdog" the next year when the store unveiled LazzieDog, complete with digital wristwatch. The bear made several return appearances in the years following, culminating in a Lazzie Millenium Bear (dressed in a tuxedo and party hat) in 1999.

Perhaps the best way to relive a Christmas at Lazarus is by viewing the 1990 movie *A Mom for Christmas*. This heartwarming tale was shot by an Australian film crew at the Lazarus-owned Shillito's store (renamed "Milliman's" for the film) in downtown Cincinnati. Produced by Walt Disney Television, it tells the story a young girl who gets her wish when a department store mannequin, played by Olivia Newton-John, comes to life. Unfortunately, it does not show as much of the store as you might like.

Chapter 13

The Beginning of the Beginning

The opening of the City Center Mall on August 18, 1989, was hailed by Mayor Dana "Buck" Rinehart as a harbinger of the rebirth of downtown Columbus. Architect and urban critic William H. Whyte wasn't so sure. Two years earlier, he had cautioned that "good downtown malls have a lot of glass that opens them up to the outside," but those that are sealed off tend to disorient the patrons. While he praised some aspects of the completed project, he admitted that he didn't like the blank western wall that faced High Street. He wasn't alone.

Malls were, essentially, full-line department stores on steroids, exploded into a number of smaller shops and boutiques. Everything once found in the downtown Lazarus store—and more—was available at the mall, just not in one place and under one management. In truth, Lazarus was already becoming something of a mall itself, with thirteen departments, ranging from "carpet cleaning and customer home furnishings to optical and shoe repair," leased to outside vendors. More were planned.

When the City Center Mall sailed into town, the flagship Lazarus store was foundering. If the mall hadn't come along when it did, it is likely that the downtown store would have been abandoned within a few years. Instead, a lifeline was cast across High Street in the form of a bridge at the second-floor level, tying it to the 1,250,000-square-feet mother ship. Sales jumped 40 percent during the first year.

"Many generations…have grown up with this store," remarked John D. Miller, the new chairman of Lazarus. "So the nostalgia, the feeling that you have a circus with two hundred acts under one roof, is something that should be preserved if at all possible." However, he hinted that there would be changes, beginning with the closing of the sixth floor, the annex and the three garages. And while he didn't mention it, the role of ringmaster was being passed to the mall manager.

Besides Lazarus, anchoring the mall were Marshall Field's and Jacobson's, two of the most respected names in retailing. However, the clock was winding down on them, too. Marshall Field's would become Kaufmann's in 2003 and Macy's two years later following Federated's acquisition of the May Company. Meanwhile, Jacobson's would go belly up in 2002, resulting in the closure of all its outlets.

Meanwhile, down I-71 in Cincinnati, a new Lazarus Furniture Gallery was opened in the former Kenwood Mall. There were forty-three Lazarus stores already, so it is arguable whether this addition was a well-reasoned decision or another act of desperation as management struggled to keep the ship aright. Although it is estimated that Lazarus earned a profit of $120 million for the year, this was before interest payment on debt, taxes and so on put them in the red.

As Adrienne Bosworth of *Columbus Monthly* pointed out, there was no celebration when sometime during the evening of Saturday, January 13, 1990, an anonymous customer spent the one billionth dollar of the fiscal year. This milestone in Lazarus history was quickly overshadowed by another less than forty-eight hours later when its parent company, Campeau Corporation, filed for bankruptcy. Looking back over four decades, Lola Hasson concluded that if you weren't having fun working at Lazarus, you simply weren't paying attention. "I couldn't wait to get to work," she said. "I was single, and I could have gone anywhere. I had all kinds of other offers, but they were so wonderful to work for…They respected you, and of course, we respected them." But "they" had changed—and not for the better.

In 1991, the Rike Kumler Company flagship store in Dayton closed after taking on the Lazarus name and was later demolished to make way for a performing arts center. Rike's traced its beginnings back to a dry goods store founded in 1853. Meanwhile, its Upper Valley Mall outlet in Springfield underwent the full rebranding and continued to operate as a Macy's.

Two Grand Rapids, Michigan Herplosheimer's stores went out of business in 1992 after being brought under the Lazarus umbrella five years earlier. (A "Herp's" store is glimpsed in the animated movie *The Polar Express*.)

Similarly, five Indianapolis-area William H. Block Company stores, converted to Lazarus branches the same year, soon closed as well: the downtown store at Illinois and Market in 1993, Glendale Mall in 1999,

The Beginning of the Beginning

Tippecanoe Mall (Tippecanoe) in 2002, College Mall (Bloomington) in 2003 and Markland Mall (Kokomo) in 2005 after becoming Macy's.

Northgate Mall (Cincinnati) got a Lazarus in 1993, while Florence Mall (Florence, Kentucky), acquired a Lazarus Home Store and the Mall at Fairfield Commons (Beavercreek, Ohio), an upscale Lazarus, both in 1994. All were rebranded Lazarus-Macy's/Macy's.

Pittsburgh-based Joseph Horne Company, founded in 1849, was one of the oldest department stores in the country. Though little known outside Pennsylvania, few of its customers embraced the chain's acquisition by Lazarus in 1994. The stores affected were Millcreek Mall (Erie), West Erie Plaza (Erie), Greengate Mall (Hempfield), Beaver Valley Mall (Monaca), Century III Mall (West Mifflin), Penn Avenue and Stanwix Street (Pittsburgh), Ross Park Mall (Pittsburgh), South Hills Village (Pittsburgh), South Hills Furniture Galley (Pittsburgh), Heights Plaza Shopping Center (Natrona), Monroeville Mall (Monroeville) and Fifth Avenue and Wood Street (Pittsburgh).

Lazarus only occupied the Penn Avenue store for one year before moving into a "glitzy" new building on Fifth Avenue. The first free-standing department store constructed in downtown Pittsburgh in twenty-five years, it won awards for its design but did not survive beyond 2004 after sales dropped 35 percent. Apparently, Quaker pride wasn't transferable, either. Millcreek, West Erie, Greengate and Beaver Valley were boarded up in 1997–98; Century III in 2001; Fifth Avenue in 2004; and Ross Park in 2006. Both South Hills stores experienced full rebranding.

Monroeville Mall was "famous" as the site of the 1978 horror film *Dawn of the Dead*, written and directed by Pittsburgh's George A. Romero. In the movie, Romero shows mindless zombies continuing to shop in the mall, loading up carts with unneeded merchandise while Muzak plays over the public address system. "What are they doing? Why do they come here?" a character in the film asks, only to be told, "Some kind of instinct. Memory, of what they used to do. This was an important place in their lives."

Buoyed by the comeback of its downtown store, Lazarus renovated its branches at Eastland, Westland and Kingsdale. It also opened a store at the Mall at Tuttle Crossing (Columbus) and at Fountain Place (Cincinnati) in 1997, as well as at Polaris Fashion Place and Easton Town Center (both Columbus) in 2001. The Easton store was intended as a prototype for future stores, but there would be no others. All of them became Lazarus-Macy's/Macy's.

The storied history of the Lazarus flagship store finally came to an end, not with a bang—or a whimper—but with a prolonged clearance sale, concluding on August 14, 2004. Sales manager Janet Fraime made the final announcement over the store intercom, "It is now 5:00 p.m., and the downtown location is closed. Thanks for your support." Only fifty employees were left to witness the end of a great adventure.

When rumors of the closing had begun to circulate less than a year earlier, John Rosenberger, executive director of Capitol South Community Urban Redevelopment Corporation, had dismissed suggestions that the loss of Lazarus would drive a stake through the mall's heart: "[My] prediction is that six months or one year or two years from now, we'll conclude it was the beginning of the beginning." Of course, Capitol South had created the City Center Mall.

In retrospect, a gang-related shooting at the City Center Mall during the spring of 1994 may have been the start of the downward spiral (although peak occupancy had actually occurred two years earlier). At least six shots were fired, and a fifteen-year-old youth had died. It was a terrifying experience for those who survived the hail of bullets and raised concerns throughout the community about the safety of mall patrons.

A year after the downtown store closed, Federated dropped the Lazarus name from the remaining thirty-six Lazarus-Macy's stores, writing it out of history like a deposed dictator. Apparently, that had been the idea all along when Federated bought R.H. Macy & Company, but it took management ten years to accomplish it.

The Macy's name was felt to have more cachet than Lazarus, Burdines, Bon Marche, Rich's or Goldsmith's, due to *Miracle on 34ᵗʰ Street*, the annual Thanksgiving Day parade and similar media exposure. However, as an editorial in *Business First* pointed out, "Central Ohio consumers likely will lament the elimination of local flavor in a sector where homogenization dominates and has made the department retailing experience ever more dull." They did and they still do.

In 2006, the Eastland Mall Macy's moved from the old Lazarus anchor store to a Kaufmann's that had opened just six months earlier. A year later, the former Lazarus-Macy's building was torn down to make way for the construction of a new J.C. Penney.

On July 31, 2007, the City of Columbus filed a lawsuit to evict Simon Property Group, managers of the City Center Mall, for neglecting to pay rent and real estate taxes, among other things. At the last minute, an agreement was reached for the city to buy the property. Kaufmann's, the last surviving anchor, was closed late the same year due to plummeting sales.

A handful of shops limped along for a year or so more. Finally, on March 5, 2009, City Center Mall was closed, too, falling victim to such suburban developments as the mall at Tuttle Crossing, Easton Town Center and Polaris Fashion Place. The $165 million tax-funded development had lasted all of twenty years.

Even before its slow death, new mall construction nationwide had nearly come to a halt. Industry analysts attribute this to the double whammy of overbuilding and online shopping. As a result, vacancy levels at U.S. malls are approaching record highs.

The City of Columbus was subsequently given the old Lazarus building, and then it purchased four adjoining acres from Federated Department Stores for $5.7 million. It had not been, as John Rosenberger boldly predicted, the beginning of the beginning. It was most definitely the end.

Chapter 14

It Was a Retail Oz

How did the great merchant families of Columbus get along? "Like brothers," according to Don Levy in an interview with the Columbus Jewish Historical Society. There was always "great camaraderie between the Lazaruses, the Levys, and the Gundersheimers."

Although they were competitors, they either felt that the town was big enough for all or that they occupied different niches like birds sharing a tree. Certainly, each of their stores—Lazarus, the Union and the Fashion—had a distinctly different feel if not an entirely different clientele. They had also traveled different roads to success and played different roles in the capital fashion scene.

In 1881, Charles Richardson Martens came to Columbus to join his brother's firm, Weisman & Martens, a dry goods store. It was thirty years after Simon Lazarus did much the same thing. Eleven years later, Charles founded the Home Store. Meanwhile, Max Morehouse, after operating retail stores in Elyria, Lorain, Findlay and Toledo, came to Columbus in 1899.

Joining forces with Charles Martens, Morehouse opened Bowland, Morehouse & Martens Company in 1907 at 130–134 South High Street. A postcard shows that it offered a cloak and suit section, silks and a French room. The following year, the name was simplified to Morehouse Martens.

Described as either a dry goods store or a department store, Morehouse Martens catered more toward the carriage trade with its high-priced, high-quality merchandise. It purportedly housed the first professionally staffed beauty salon in the city.

On November 7, 1910, Max Morehouse commissioned the first commercial air freight when he hired pilot Philip O. Parmalee to transport two bolts of silk from Dayton to Columbus, landing at Driving Park on the east side. The sixty-five-mile flight took sixty-six minutes. It was strictly a publicity stunt.

The Fashion was founded in 1912 by Allen Gundersheimer Sr. and Max H. Rieser. Originally located at the northwest corner of State and High Streets, it was later moved south, directly opposite Lazarus. In 1948, Allied Stores, the owners of Morehouse Martens, bought it out because it wanted to expand its store, located immediately to the north. Two years later, Allied physically connected the two stores by bridging the narrow alley that separated them. The merged store was renamed Morehouse-Fashion, later shortened to the Fashion.

When the Fashion went out of business, the Union (founded by Saul M. Levy, grandfather of Allen Gundersheimer Jr.) moved south to occupy the vacated building. It, in turn, was bought out by Marshall Field's and was operated out of Cleveland as a Halle's store until it went bankrupt.

Max Morehouse was also the brother-in-law of Charles Anson Bond, founder of Bond Clothes and president of Religious Pictures, Inc. In 1901, Bond came to Columbus with his wife and family and promptly opened a men's clothing shop at 237 North High Street. Later, he served as mayor of Columbus (1908–9), only to have his wife die in childbirth within weeks of his election.

Upon completion of his term, Bond started the first national chain of men's clothing stores. His shop at 46 North High Street was one of the first in the city to have a neon sign. An illuminated waterfall sign on the Times Square store in New York City was featured in many movies and newsreels shot during the 1940s. The Bond chain was finally liquidated in 1974.

Founded by the Saul M. Levy, the Union—"the Home of Quality"—was opened at the northwest corner of Long and North High Streets in 1894. It was called the Union because it had started in Chicago during the Civil War, when preserving "the Union" was on everyone's mind.

While passing through Columbus in the spring of 1894, Saul had met then governor William McKinley, who suggested that he consider the city as a site for a store. Saul agreed that it was a good idea, and they became fast friends. Nine years after it opened, the Union was destroyed by a fire on April 26, 1903. It was quickly rebuilt as a two-story store. Although it originally carried only a men's line, it was expanded to include women's clothing in 1910. A six-story addition was completed in 1923.

In 1947, the Union became the first major store in Columbus to open a branch when it built a small store on Lane Avenue in Upper Arlington. After undergoing several expansions, it was moved to Kingsdale Shopping

Center in 1959. As early as 1954, the Union had also opened a store at Graceland Shopping Center. Soon, it was to build stores in Chillicothe, Marion and Lancaster as well. At one time, the chain consisted of fifteen stores throughout Ohio and West Virginia.

Lazarus had increasingly become the locus of downtown shopping, so after the Fashion building became available in 1968, the Union moved into it to take advantage of the location. However, the Levys no longer owned the company by this time, having sold it to Manhattan Industry, makers of Manhattan shirts.

The *Columbus Dispatch* reported that the new store had an elegant décor that featured "plush crushed velvet on many walls and a fourth-floor 'Street of Shops' that included a Peddler's Villa gift shop, an International House of greeting cards and wrappings, a French crystal and china shop, and a patio restaurant decorated in black-and-white hounds-tooth checks." In the opinion of Doral Chenoweth, the Union's Terrace Room was the "last tea room of note" in the city.

About 1980, Marshall Field's bought the Union stores from Manhattan Industry and assigned Cleveland-based Halle's to run them. This arrangement failed miserably. Jerome Schottenstein, former chairman of Schottenstein Stores Corporation, bought Halle's from Marshall Field Company in November 1981. The intent was to operate the Union stores under the Halle's brand. However, only two month later, he announced that he was going to close them because they were unprofitable. He sold the Kingsdale branch, the only one still open, to a former Halle's executive, who revived the Union name. This store finally closed in 1994, a victim of City Center Mall's popularity.

In 1903, Hirsch Kobacker, a Lithuanian Jew, opened a dry goods store in Mount Pleasant, Pennsylvania. A couple of years later, he ran a cloak and millinery store in Connesville before eventually making his way to Columbus, where he and his sons purchased the Boston Store in 1919. It was started years earlier by Federman and Levy, who operated a chain of similar establishments throughout the Midwest.

As early as 1921, Hirsch, age sixty-two, and his sons Jerome, thirty-six, and Alfred J., thirty-four, were opening branch stores in Buffalo, New York. Three years later, they moved their Columbus store into the former Columbus Dry Goods Company building, tripling the size of their operation.

It was an impressive addition to an already crowded field. The Boston Store emphasized, "We are the youngest big store among you, but there is an old saying: THAT YOUTH MUST BE SERVED." The renovated and enlarged five-story edifice included a "soda grill"—a liquid automated refrigerating fountain that used neither ice nor salt (unlike the old Niagara unit at Lazarus).

While the Boston Store name popped up all over the country and was used by at least four unrelated chains, the Kobacker's operated three stores locally: downtown, Town & Country Shopping Center (1952) and Northern Lights Shopping Center (1955). The family quickly became known for their philanthropy.

Alfred J. Kobacker, who was born in 1924, managed the Boston Store chain following his graduation from Yale University in 1945. However, he soon shifted his focus to shoes, opening his first shoe store in 1960. A year later, the Boston Store merged with New York's Federal (not Federated) Department Stores, which went bankrupt a decade afterward.

Despite the poor state of the economy, life and business went on. In 1930, Louis and Jean Madison moved from Cleveland to Columbus, where they opened Madison's, a women's specialty store, at 72 North High Street. Naturally, Louis tried to learn what he could from his competition. Every Sunday morning, he and his son, David, would go downtown to study the display windows at Lazarus.

During the 1940s, Louis expanded his operations by opening branch stores in Akron, Mansfield and Lima. A Madison's store was part of the original Kingsdale Shopping Center development in 1959, even as the three branch stores were being phased out. Additional stores followed at Town & Country Shopping Center, at the Northland, Eastland and Westland Malls and at Worthington Square. However, the volume of business at the downtown store declined as a direct result. The family finally sold the stores in 1991, but David had quit the business long before that. Instead, he became mayor of Bexley for the next thirty-two years.

And then there was Schottenstein's. In the early 1900s, Ephraim L. Schottenstein immigrated to Columbus, where other members of his family had already settled. After three years of selling clothing and fruit from a horse and buggy, he opened a store on Parsons Avenue at Reeb in 1912.

Schottenstein had been born in Kurland, Latvia. The original family name was Jagetsy, but they changed it to Schottenstein while still in Europe. In 1930, the store was moved to 1887 Parsons Avenue, not far from Buckeye Steel Castings, where it became a fixture on the city's south side.

Despite its notoriously uneven floors, this ramshackle building became the cornerstone of the Schottenstein empire. During the next decade, Ephraim noticed that there was a growing demand for furniture, so he began selling it out of the basement of his store. After World War II, sales soared, so in 1946 he formed Schottenstein Stores Corporation to operate both a department store and a furniture business. Eventually, Value City Furniture was spun off as a separate entity.

The original Schottenstein's was closed in 2005. For almost ninety-three years, it had been the "bargain" department store, catering to the blue-collar residents of what had once been called Steelton. The surprise announcement left many workers and neighbors "shocked," as Tracy Turner reported in the *Columbus Dispatch*. One in particular, Juanita Lambert, age seventy-five, had worked at the southside institution for forty-seven years.

Mike Harden of the *Dispatch* covered its closing. "The neighborhood was a stew of Hungarians, Italians, Slovenians and Croatians," he wrote. "Appalachians arrived daily, winnowed from the hamlets and played-out mines of Kentucky, West Virginia and southern Ohio." For many of them, who had been accustomed to shopping with company scrip at company-owned stores, "It was a retail Oz." To regular customer Tom Belcher, "It was the poor man's Lazarus."

From the original Lazarus to the "poor man's Lazarus," all of these great retailers have now, regrettably, faded from the scene.

Chapter 15

Life After Lazarus

The summer after Tony Cox moved to the United States, his parents came from the United Kingdom to visit. After giving them a grand tour of Columbus, his mother said, "Well, I understand that Toys "R" Us is a toy store, but I cannot fathom what that big Laz-R-Us shop is selling." She was clearly "having a laugh," but the time will come when hardly anyone will know what the big Lazarus shop was selling. And that's a pity.

Of the more than five thousand publicly traded U.S. companies, fewer than 10 percent are 100 years or older. The odds that any of them will equal or surpass 150 years are staggering, but that's exactly what Lazarus did.

According to Vicki TenHaken, professor of management at Hope College, companies that survive for a century or more have big goals that keep their employees motivated through the decades. Furthermore, they are innovative but careful; they don't take huge risks on untested ideas. Finally, they are financially conservative, resisting the temptation to load up on debt. That was Lazarus; it wasn't Campeau.

In 1957, Fred Lazarus Jr. addressed the Newcomen Society of Cincinnati about his life's passion, retailing:

> *Let us assume that in the course of a millennium, our civilization has been surpassed and lies buried, like the seven cities of Troy. Let us picture to ourselves…some future archaeologist who, digging in the ruins…comes upon remains of a department store! A department store would give our archaeologist materials for a lifetime of well-founded conjecture…He could deduce, with reasonable accuracy, what was precious to us, what*

we considered necessary, the things we worked for, the fabric of our day-to-day lives.

Of course, no future archaeologist will get that opportunity. The department store of which Uncle Fred spoke no longer exists. Oh, there are still enterprises bearing such fabled names as Macy's, Bloomingdale's and Filene's (basement only), but they are mere shadows of the grand emporiums that once graced the downtowns of most cities worthy of the name. Their ghosts still haunt such economically devastated landscapes as Cleveland (Higbee's), St. Louis (Stix, Baer & Fuller) and Chicago (Carson, Pirie, Scott), standing empty and forlorn.

What made Lazarus great was built on a business model for another day. In the end, Lazarus, like many of its Federated brethren, found itself stuck with an oversized building in an inconvenient location. The executives hung on to the flagship store as long as they could, longer than they should have (in the opinion of a surprisingly unsentimental Mr. Charles), before finally letting go.

All Lazarus males through the third generation had embarked on careers in the family store. But by the fourth, a few had begun to drift away; most of the fifth never even signed on. In fact, they were discouraged from entering the business, according to David Lazarus, because it wasn't felt to be "healthy." There was thought to be too much nepotism.

"It was no longer a place where four brothers could run it and have a good time," explained Stuart Lazarus, son of Charles. "It was too large, too overreaching and it just didn't seem right for me." Besides, the Lazarus heirs had the luxury of being able to choose to do whatever they wanted for a living, knowing that their family's affluence would sustain them.

The impact of Lazarus on Columbus, on Ohio and on the nation went far beyond the store's economic footprint. The belief that community involvement was good for business led members of the family to take leading roles in matters of social conscience and public welfare. Sometimes they were out front leading the charge, and at other times they worked behind the scenes, but throughout the store's history they did not hesitate to use their influence and money to make their hometown a better place.

In the aftermath of the 1913 flood, Uncle Fred and Uncle Si campaigned for the construction of the Scioto River levee and the Civic Center government complex. At the end of World War I, members of the Lazarus family helped found the Community Chest (and Mr. Charles later led the first United Appeal drive in 1951). Uncle Jack created the Camp Lazarus

Boy Scout Camp in 1925. To honor the store's centennial, Lazarus donated $100,000 to purchase a building on East State Street to house the United Community Council. Uncle Bob served on the Metropolitan Committee, which directed most civic development decisions during the 1940s and 1950s.

Mr. Bob's role in the company was, essentially, to do good, so his name will be found attached to such groups as the chamber of commerce, Urban League, Columbus Youth Foundation, Friends of the Drexel, King Arts Complex, Columbus College of Art and Design, Son of Heaven Commission, Council for Ethics in Economics and Ballet Met. If anything, his wife, Mary, is even better known for her dedication to numerous boards and causes.

Over the years, Lazarus women chaired various organizations, from the League of Women Voters to the District Nursing Association. They were active in the Red Cross, Children's Hospital, Columbus Society for the Prevention and Cure of Tuberculosis, Baby Camp, Mothers Health Association, ProMusica, Women's Fund of Central Ohio, Columbus Museum of Art, Columbus Symphony Orchestra, city council and many others.

According to Char Witkind, all four of the third-generation brothers were members of Temple Israel, but only Simon was truly active. Char, in fact, described her father, Uncle Bob, as an "areligious" man. He disagreed with the Schottensteins, who closed their stores on Saturdays to observe the Jewish Sabbath. He considered himself a merchant first, and if his customers wanted the store open, it should be open.

Even though many members of the family have married outside the Jewish faith, and some have even said that they feel more comfortable in a church than a temple, Bob Lazarus Jr. expressed the wish that his family would be remembered for the values they brought to the business of retailing—values rising out of their Jewish heritage. He felt that Lazarus always stood for the principle that all people should be treated fairly and honestly.

In summing up the importance of American department stores, Jan Whittaker declared: "They brought beauty and pleasure into the lives of a nation of pragmatic, almost stoical people. They provided services to the broad masses that had once been reserved for elites. They became the stewards of the middle class, shaping, cultivating, and enshrining its aspirations and way of life." Food for thought at a time when some believe the middle class itself is endangered.

Fortunately, the downtown Lazarus store did not fall to the wrecking ball and may not for years to come. Instead, it was converted into what has been hailed as "the most significant 'green' building in the country." More than

The newly renovated Lazarus building is the Midwest's largest "green" project. *PC.*

75 percent of the structure was preserved during its redevelopment, and a rooftop garden was installed to harvest water for cooling the building. Upon its completion, the project was award a Gold certification through the LEED (Leadership in Energy and Environmental Design) rating system.

More importantly, the former Lazarus store provides space for up to 2,600 jobs. Among the initial tenants are a number of city, county and state government offices, as well as the Columbus Chamber of Commerce and the Ohio State University Urban Arts spaces, with the promise of a coffee shop and a bank branch to come. Perhaps the repurposed building will provide an economic stimulus to the downtown in much the way the F&R Lazarus & Company did during its heyday. At least, we can always hope.

"A department store," Robert Sr. once said, "is a living mirror of our civilization in which we see the constantly changing needs and wishes of our people." Sadly, that mirror has been shattered, and we now must look elsewhere to view our reflection.

Postscript: As with most buildings that have any age to them, the downtown Lazarus store is supposedly haunted by the ghost of its founder, Simon Lazarus (and a couple of anonymous others). He has been "seen" looking out the first-floor windows at night. Not a particularly imaginative tale as ghost stories go, but one that begs the question of why his spirit would be tied to a piece of real estate that meant nothing to him during his lifetime. Perhaps he doesn't remember that the store he founded was located across the street.

Appendix I
The Federated Juggernaut

In November 1929, only a month following the "Black Thursday" stock market crash, Fred Lazarus Jr. orchestrated the merger of several family-owned department stores under the banner of Federated Department Stores, Inc. His objective was to diversify risk through mutual ownership of one another's stock. No attempt was made to centralize control, purchasing, planning or evaluation.

Earlier in the year, one of Fred Jr.'s sons had been run down by an automobile. While still mourning the boy's death, the Lazarus vice-president met with three other prominent merchants on a yacht in Long Island Sound: Louis Kirstein of Boston's Filene's, Samuel Bloomingdale of New York's Bloomingdale's and Simon Rothschild of Brooklyn's Abraham & Straus. He, of course, spoke for F&R Lazarus & Company of Columbus and Lazarus-owned John Shillito's of Cincinnati.

"Under the proposed plan of affiliating through a common holding company," his brother, Simon, later assured Columbus shoppers, "the individual character and local identity of the participating stores will in no way be affected." However, they expected to realize joint buying economies and pass the savings on to their customers.

By the time of his own death in 1973, Fred Lazarus Jr. had been acknowledged as one of the true giants in his field. The grandson of the dynasty's founder, Fred had an inauspicious start. As a child, he (barely) survived bouts of scarlet fever and measles, leaving him with a residual tremor in his hand. He grew up in the family business, beginning in the collar department. For a few months, he attended Ohio State University before dropping out to work full-time in the store.

Although small of stature, Uncle Fred had big ideas. Among his innovations was the introduction of "accounts receivable," the bookkeeping convention by which merchandise that had been sold, but not yet paid for, was posted in the ledger as an asset. Every other merchant quickly followed his lead.

However, Fred had something far more ambitious in mind. Inspired by John D. Rockefeller's Standard Oil Trust, he urged the other merchant princes assembled on Rothschild's yacht to pool their interests in a holding company. By consolidating their resources, they would be even stronger and in a better position to weather the upcoming economic depression.

Federated Department Stores was a logical extension of the Retail Research Association, masterminded by Lincoln Filene. All stores would be under common ownership while retaining their own identities and methods of operation. Abraham Lincoln Filene, age sixty-four, was elected president.

Headquartered in Columbus, Federated proved itself during the first year of operation when its net income more than tripled its fixed expenses. However, according to author John Rothschild in *Going for Broke*, initially it served as little more than "a glorified lobbying group for the four founding members."

By the '40s, Fred was regretting how the original deal had been structured. The Lazarus family had received fewer shares in Federated because Lazarus and Shillito's represented smaller markets. However, since they dominated those markets in a way the others did not, their profits were being redistributed as dividends to the other shareholders. Unfortunately, there was nothing he could do about it.

When Lincoln Filene moved up to chairman in 1945, Fred was tapped to succeed him as president of Federated. He immediately decided to move the company to Cincinnati. Ostensibly, he was concerned that if he remained in Columbus he would "butt heads" with the leadership of Lazarus. He also wanted to keep a closer watch over Shillito's, which was being run by his youngest brother, Jeffrey.

According to Jeffrey Lazarus Jr., "When the headquarters left the mother church in Columbus, it was a terrible slap in the face to the family in Columbus." It also signaled the transfer of the family power base to the Queen City.

Fred Jr. quickly locked horns with Samuel Joseph Bloomingdale over the issue of a bonus plan. He felt that Federated should pay—with stock options—for the work that he and his brothers would be performing on its behalf. Ultimately, Uncle Fred prevailed when the stockholders sided with him. He set to work at once to establish an acquisitions department.

The Federated Juggernaut

Toward the end of the war, Fred visited his son in Houston, where he was stationed with the U.S. Army Air Force. Impressed with the city's potential, he returned to Cincinnati and persuaded the other board members that they should enter the south Texas market. With this move, Federated was transformed from a holding company to an operating company.

Fred Jr. first made an offer on the Foley Brothers Dry Goods Company. When the Houston firm said that it wasn't interested, he bought some property and announced his intention to open his own store. Fearing that it wouldn't be able to compete with this interloper, Foley's agreed to sell out for $4,300,000.

Next, Fred set about testing his theory that department stores would only be able to survive if they mechanized. He hired Raymond Loewy, the "Father of Industrial Design," to design a store that would be more efficient. The result was a $13 million windowless, glass-walled building interlaced with chutes and conveyor belts—the most modern store in the country. Customers would park in a Foley garage, make purchases in the Foley store, eat in the Foley restaurant and find everything waiting for them in their cars at the end of the day. The very fact that Foley's was now part of Federated doubled sales during the first year.

Over the next couple of decades, Uncle Fred undertook a campaign to build a nationwide empire through strategic acquisitions. While many of these were in large cities, he believed that the department store's future was in the medium-sized ones. Although in his sixties, he was not nearly ready for retirement. Within ten years, Federated became the nation's largest retailer, with a network of thirty-eight stores doing more than $500 million in sales yearly.

Under Fred's leadership, Federated brought the following stores into the fold: Halliburton's (Oklahoma City), Sanger Brothers and A. Harris & Company (Dallas), Boston Store (Milwaukee), Burdines (Miami), Rike's (Dayton), Goldsmith's (Memphis), Bullock's (Los Angeles) and I. Magnin (San Francisco).

It took a federal antitrust suit in the mid-1960s to "slow the Federated juggernaut," according to an article in *Cincinnati* magazine. Nevertheless, Rich's of Atlanta was added to the roster in 1976. Since Fred Jr. could no longer tour his empire by car, the Federated Air Force—four airplanes, eight pilots and three assistants—ferried company executives around the country.

Fred Jr. once enumerated some of his basic retailing principles for *Kiplinger* magazine:

- "Keep a big variety of stock"—Make the typical housewife believe she can get everything she wants at your store.
- "Watch timing"—Ensure you have the items on hand before the customer wants them.
- "Compete at least a little with everybody"—Don't concede tools to Sears or jewelry to Tiffany's.
- "Don't give buyers too much to do"—Keep their departments small and their territory limited so they can spend time on the road buying things.
- "Work tirelessly to get scarce items"—Shillito's buyers scoured the country during a candy shortage to ensure they had stock when others didn't.
- "Feel real responsibility to your customers"—Federated store restaurants had stayed open and operated at a loss when food was scarce.
- "Never treat complaints casually"—One complaint wipes out profit on four to eight sales.
- "Service is more than a smile"—Serve the best possible chocolate sodas and at least three minutes faster than the competition.
- "Keep decentralized"—Each department head should be allowed to run his own show.
- "Lean on business forecasts"—Watch business indexes and supplement them with your own studies.
- "Analyze markets"—Use available data to search for new opportunities.[22]
- "Never stop studying methods"—Look for ways to improve everything.[23]
- "Keep training employees"—Identify potential so you can promote from within.

In 1951, Ralph Lazarus left his job as vice-president and general merchandise manager at Lazarus and moved to Cincinnati to become executive vice-president of Federated. Fred Jr.'s other two sons, Fred III and Maurice ("Mogie"), joined him, the former as chairman of Shillito's and the latter as chief financial officer of Federated before becoming president of Filene's.

As price wars were breaking out in New York, Fred Jr. made headlines when he told stockholders that employing loss-leaders to draw customers to the store was a "destructive" merchandising strategy. He argued that it hurts local distributors, manufacturers and "tens of thousands of small retailers who perform a real service to their communities."

Owing to various fair trade laws, the first discount stores were considered by many to be "outlaw" operations. Enacted during the 1920s, state and federal statutes allowed manufacturers to "fix" the prices of their merchandise without running afoul of antitrust laws. If a vendor sold an item for less than the suggested retail price, then a manufacturer could refuse to sell to them. However, discount stores began circumventing this restriction by selling the items for 20 to 30 percent less while introducing their own private brands.

Fair trade laws had come to be viewed by many as anything but fair and certainly not beneficial to trade. They also violated the spirit of competition. Most manufacturers had lost interest in enforcing the laws, so discount stores began to thrive. The traditional department stores were forced to drop their prices as well.

In 1967, Lazarus/Federated started the Columbus-based Gold Circle chain of discount stores. The company acquired the Richway chain of discount stores in 1976 and combined it with Gold Circle ten years later. In 1982, Federated bought Twin Fair, Inc., a discount chain based in Buffalo, New York, and merged it with Gold Circle as well. It was a far different world than the one the F&R Lazarus & Company had been born and grew up in, and things would only get worse.

Ralph Lazarus, Fred Jr.'s son, succeeded him as president of Federated in 1957, while Fred moved up to chairman and Lincoln Filene became honorary chairman. However, according to Rothschild, Ralph "was reportedly more attracted to pomp than to profit margins, and Federated muddled through the 1970s in a secure but undistinguished way." Consequently, the company fell out of favor with Wall Street.

During his tenure, Ralph achieved some unexpected fame courtesy of WLW television's *Paul Dixon Show*. Dixon had introduced a "Mystery Voice Contest." He would call someone at random from the local phone book, play a recording of a voice and ask the contestant if he or she could identify who it was.

Incredibly, the very first contestant immediately identified the "Mystery Voice" as Ralph Lazarus. Stunned, Dixon asked the woman how she could possibly have known. She explained with a laugh that she had once been Ralph's private secretary.[24]

In 1979, Howard Goldfeder took over Federated's reins and set about consolidating divisions. He was responsible for opening several new Filene's Basements, purchasing the Children's Palace toy chain, expanding Bloomingdale's outside New York and establishing MainStreet, the moderately priced clothing store chain. All of these ventures were disappointments, setting the stage for Robert Campeau to swoop in.

Bob, as everyone called him, was a Canadian real estate developer who had just taken over Allied Stores, seemingly on a whim (or, perhaps, out of spite). In 1986, he set his sights on Federated, tendering an offer of forty-seven dollars per share. Few took him seriously, given the lowball price, the fact that he was not aligned with any bank and his insistence that he be given four months to complete the transaction following negotiations.

One of thirteen children born in the mining town of Sudbury, Bob had dropped out of school at fourteen. When he was twenty-five, he sold a home that he had built and realized a profit of $3,000. Within the year, he had built and sold forty more homes on his way to becoming a "blue-collar billionaire." He firmly believed that "[y]ou have to push yourself to the front of the line" and clearly had no compunctions about doing so.

Only a few months earlier, Bob Campeau had reneged on his assurance that he did not "intend to sell Allied's assets to pay for the transaction," dumping sixteen of twenty-four divisions and laying off four thousand store employees. His demonstrated method of operation was to slash expenses in order to pay down his debt. No one believed that this time would be any different.

Even as Bob bumped up his offer, Federated's lawyers and local politicians sprung into action, hoping to stop the corporate raider dead in his tracks. People began sporting "Say No to Campeau" buttons (a maple leaf with a red line through it). But Bob had a legal team of his own, waging war in the courts of Delaware, Florida, South Carolina, Nebraska, New York and, of course, Ohio.

Along the way, Bob picked up the support of Youngstown shopping center developer Edward J. DeBartolo. Earlier, Allied had offered DeBartolo $57 million if he would simply place a higher bid than Campeau for Allied Stores. DeBartolo did, took the money and then turned around and loaned $150 million to Bob so that he could make an even higher counteroffer. This proved to be the takeover bid. And now Bob and Ed were at it again.

Meanwhile, R.H. Macy & Company entered the game, driving the price of Federated even higher. It quickly became obvious to everyone that the "winner" would be forced to liquidate some company assets simply to reduce the enormous debt. Finally, a truce was arranged between Campeau and Macy's. Bob would purchase Federated for $73.50 a share in cash and sell three Federated divisions to Macy's for $1.1 billion, and Macy's would also receive $60 million to pay off its bankers and lawyers.

The Federated Juggernaut

On April 13, 1988, Campeau was scheduled to pay a visit to the downtown Lazarus store. Bob Lazarus Jr. was waiting for him at the Front Street entrance when a customer asked a clerk to show him how to tie the bowtie he had just purchased. The clerk couldn't and turned to Mr. Bob for assistance. The executive vice-president, who always said that he was never too busy to help a customer, proceeded to demonstrate just as Campeau's limousine pulled up outside. Jack Wiley of the *Columbus Dispatch* subsequently mused in his column, "Wonder if Campeau noticed."

When Campeau took control of Federated in 1988, all that remained were Bloomingdale's, Abraham & Straus, Rich's, Lazarus, Burdines and Goldsmith's. He immediately set about slashing the budget by $240 million. Pinks slips were sent out, eliminating some 3,400 employees—at least until it was realized that some of them were actually needed.

Many of Bob's initial decisions were reversed within a few months. Equipment had to be repurchased, data bases rebuilt and departments reestablished because too little thought had been given to the impact of these cuts. Federated's new boss was as extravagant as he was penny-pinching. Although it was imperative that they cut expenses and maximize cash flow in order to survive, there was no clear direction from the top.

For the nine-month period ending in January 1989, Federated lost $158 million. The following year, it filed for bankruptcy protection. How could it not? Campeau had paid $6.6 billion, some $500 million more than it was worth. It was the fourth-largest bankruptcy filing in U.S. history.

"If you truly analyze Federated," Robert Morosky, who briefly ran the company before falling out with Campeau, told Adrienne Bosworth, "every year they had a profit. But if you take a base year of 1970 and measure inflation, you see that profits were eroding. They were not keeping up."

In 1992, it emerged as a new public company following the ouster of Bob Campeau. Ironically, Macy's was coming out of bankruptcy at the same time, and Federated took it over in 1994, forming the largest department store corporation in the world. The fabled New York retailer was now headquartered in Cincinnati. A year later, Federated merged Lazarus with Atlanta-based Rich's and Goldsmith's, relocating the headquarters to Atlanta.

Federated initiated "Project Hyphen" in 2003, changing the names of all of its non-Macy's stores (save Bloomingdale's) to include the Macy's name (i.e., the Bon Marche became Bon-Macy's, Goldsmith became Goldsmith's-Macy's, Lazarus became Lazarus-Macy's and so on). A year afterward, "Project Star" reversed the process, dropping the hyphenated names in favor of just Macy's. In 2007, Federated Departments Stores was renamed Macy's, Inc. The stock ticker designation on the New York Stock Exchange changed from "FD" to "M."

By 2009, Moody's and Standard & Poor's had downgraded the debt rating of Macy's, Inc. bonds to junk status. Lazarus was gone. Federated was gone. And a golden era had ended.

Appendix II
A Bias in Favor of Department Store Dining

There was a time in the not-too-distant past when the main Lazarus store offered customers the choice of a dozen different dining options. Or maybe it was only eleven. Either way, it had as many as, if not more than, any other department store in the country. But it is for the quality, not the quantity, of these establishments that it is best remembered. People just loved the food.

One in particular, the Chintz Room, was a true destination restaurant, but many of the others had their fans, too. They had to be good because the competition was keen. Doral Chenoweth, the "Grumpy Gourmet," recalled that before World War II there were more than fifty places to eat within a four- or five-block radius of Capitol Square.

Among the most popular were Mill's Cafeteria, F.W. Woolworth Company, Kuenning's, Benny Klein's, Marzetti's, the Ringside Café, Paoletti's, Tom Johnson's, the State Restaurant, the Terrace Room (on the fourth floor of the Union) and, of course, the Buckeye and the Chintz Rooms at Lazarus. ("The Grump" also noted that the Jefferson Room at the Virginia Hotel reputedly served the worst food downtown.)

As Jan Whitaker, author of *Tea at the Blue Lantern Inn: A Social History of the Tea Room Craze in America*, pointed out:

> *In small cities—and some large ones too—restaurants in department stores were frequently the best places to eat. Often they did their own baking and made desserts from scratch. It was not unusual for them to whip up mayonnaise and produce their own potato chips. Their kitchens*

were often directed and entirely staffed by women professionally trained in restaurant management. They invariably favored home-style methods of cooking.

The first department store restaurant—a tearoom—is credited to Harry Gordon Selfridge at Chicago's Marshall Field's in April 1890. A few dry goods stores had already introduced restaurants, and Field abhorred them personally, but Selfridge was a visionary and, apparently, a persuasive manager. The South Tea Room was an immediate hit, offering such "exotic" dishes as Cleveland creamed chicken.

At the time, it was not considered proper for an unescorted woman to dine at a restaurant, so ladies who shopped at Marshall Field's would return home for lunch. However, one day, a store clerk shared her lunch—a chicken pot pie—with a hungry shopper, and the idea of an in-store restaurant room was born. To commemorate the event, Marshall Field's put Mrs. Herring's Chicken Pot Pie on the menu (although some suspect that the whole story was dreamed up by Selfridge, a promotional genius).

A year later, F&R Lazarus & Company made its initial foray into the food service field when it opened the twenty-five-seat Niagara Soda Fountain. A scoop of ice cream was a nickel, and a soda, available in eight different flavors, was a dime.

The famous Niagara Soda Fountain was installed at Lazarus in 1891, the first of many in-store dining establishments. *CML.*

A Bias in Favor of Department Store Dining

The first store in the city to provide customers with a place to eat, it was a rousing success. Other merchants soon followed suit. When Lazarus moved its operations across the street to a new building in 1909, the marble soda fountain went with it.

The advantage of in-store restaurants was obvious. Keeping hungry shoppers in the building increased the likelihood that they would continue shopping after eating. It was not unusual for women to plan a full day of shopping at Lazarus, especially with such additional enticements as entertainment and fashion shows.

By 1910, the tearoom craze reached Columbus when Lazarus was, purportedly, the first local store to open one (although a year earlier, the Beggs & Company, a rival store on State Street, was promoting a restaurant of its own). It provided a safe place for ladies to meet and socialize.

The Fifth Floor Tea Room was opened on December 2, 1914, and expanded from 150 to 400 seats within a year, occupying the entire floor. On most days, from 11:30 a.m. to 2:00 p.m., either a string quartet or a piano player provided music for dining. Occasionally, Jorg Fasting staged dance recitals. State legislators patronized the establishment so frequently that a special table was named for them.

The same year, a second tearoom was established on the first-floor balcony. As far as can be determined, these tearooms did not have any particular names at first but were instead referred to as the Balcony Tea Room and the Fifth Floor Tea Room. During the period 1914 through 1925, Lazarus opened a total of eight separate restaurants.

In 1915, according to Charlotte Witkind, Lazarus family historian, her Uncle Simon discovered a young woman, Mary Love, in Topeka, Kansas, operating a Fred Harvey Restaurant (later made famous by the Judy Garland musical *The Harvey Girls*). He was so impressed with her management abilities that he persuaded her to come to Columbus to open a tearoom in his store.

A home economics major, Love managed the tearoom until 1920, when she opened a place of her own at 112 East Broad Street. Seven years later, she moved it to 137 East Broad Street and named it the Maramor—a word created from "Mary" and "amor," the Latin word for love. The Maramor earned a national reputation after the royal couple of the American stage, Alfred Lunt and Lynn Fontaine, proclaimed it "the best restaurant in America."

In 1921, Helen A. Sawyer, a graduate of the University of Nebraska, was recruited to manage the two existing tearooms. She had previously been connected to the Columbus YWCA Cafeteria, which gave her a good

157

perspective when it came to knowing what young women would like. She had five college women as assistants and a staff of one hundred.

The challenge with the Balcony Tea Room was to increase the turnover of customers and, consequently, the volume of sales since the profit on each menu item was small. On one Saturday in the early 1920s, the Balcony Tea Room alone served 1,243 meals. Most entrees were priced from twenty-five cents to forty-five cents to make them attractive to working women.

The large Lazarus tearoom became a popular place for college sororities and alumnae groups to hold card parties, rush parties and similar social functions. The bill of fare included a variety of sandwiches, such as creamed sweetbreads on toast, black walnut relish, King Albert and the ever popular club. However, Lazarus also offered "hygienic foods" (e.g., shredded wheat).

"Some years ago when we were in Columbus," a writer for *Hotel Monthly* noted, "we were advised to see the new tea room of the Lazarus Company department store, managed by Miss Sawyer. We found at that time one of the best ordered tea rooms we had ever seen." As leader of the eight-piece Allensworth Orchestra, Kathryn Senter Allensworth enjoyed a long engagement at the tearoom during the mid-1920s.

Sometime before World War II, the company began referring to the restaurant as the Lazarus Tearoom in its advertisements, noting that a complete meal could be purchased for sixty-five cents. However, it may have

The fifth-floor Pavilion Tea Room was where women met to socialize. *CML.*

also been called the Pavilion Tea Room as early as 1926 (when the Ann Simpson Davis Chapter of the Daughters of the American Revolution was organized there). Women in white gloves and hats would ride a streetcar to the center of town and dine on Swiss steak with hash browns (fifty cents) and chocolate cream stack pie (fifteen cents).

During the war, gasoline rationing forced even more people to take streetcars. The fare was only a dime, including a transfer for the trolley, which would deliver them to the front door of Lazarus. Saturday afternoon teas became the rage, accompanied by great food served on fine china and linens. The tearoom also became the site of women's fashion shows. The store's own models would "walk the runway" among the tables of diners.

In 1953, the space previously occupied by the Fifth Floor Tea Room was extensively remodeled and reopened as the Chintz Room, an upscale restaurant named for its chintz-patterned curtains. A traditional lunch and dinner venue, it was famous for its chicken salad with pineapples and pecans, the most requested of all Lazarus recipes.

Among its other selections were scalloped eggplant, steamed celery dressing, hot bread pudding with bourbon sauce and various finger foods inspired by the cuisine of London's chic stores and hotels. Children were delighted by the upside-down ice cream cone decorated with a clown face. The Chintz Room remained the site of the store's seasonal fashion shows.

"My first independent dining experience occurred when I was 10 years old," *New York Times* food columnist Molly O'Neill recalled. "My mother gave me 50 cents, and I took the bus from our home 20 blocks south to downtown Columbus, Ohio, and had lunch in the tea room of Lazarus, the department store. I remember the meal in exquisite detail: a dainty plate of chicken dressing with giblet gravy accompanied by a glass of milk. It was perfect. Even today, slabs of perfect foie gras and glasses of 1921 Chateau d'Yquem don't always surpass the memory I reserve for that first taste of self-determination. And I may still have a bias in favor of department-store dining."

"Lazarus was home to many fine restaurants," Jennifer Hambrick wrote in the *Short North Gazette*, "but I remember the Chintz Room for its hostess who, it seemed, had worked there forever. She was middle aged and wore her hair in an impeccable beehive that matched the formality of her jacket and skirt. With military precision, she would hold up the same number of fingers as there were people in your party. A businesslike flick of the wrist signaled you to follow her to your table." The restaurant finally closed on January 30, 1998, after forty-five years of service.

In 1926, the Balcony Tea Room was replaced by the Colonial Room. A coffee shop designed to resemble Williamsburg's Raleigh Tavern, it offered a full-line menu that included chicken salad lemonaise, steamed celery dressing and a baked potato encrusted in rock salt. Although it was closed in 1995, the Colonial Room was reopened three years later as a 120-seat restaurant, catering to the employees of the recently repurposed building. Many of its recipes were later rolled out to other restaurants in the stores.

The Lazarus Pepsi Bar was opened in 1945. Located in the Hi-Jinx Room of the second-floor High School Shop, it was intended as a place for teenage girls to meet in much the same way the tearooms were for their mothers. They could come and discuss fashion with members of the Hi-School Board (selected female students from area high schools who modeled new

The Hi-Jinx Room, opened in 1945, was for teenage girls what the tearooms were for their mothers. *PC.*

clothing in the store). They could also meet celebrities such as WBNS radio deejay Irwin "Early Bird" Johnson or movie and stage star Gene Sheldon (a Columbus native). Vocalist Eddie Metzger from Bexley High School served as master of ceremonies.

One of the most frequented restaurants in the store was the twenty-five-thousand-square-feet, 1,500-seat Associates' Cafeteria with its eighty-six-foot-long serving line. It was located on the second floor of the building at South Front and West Town Streets. Because it was restricted to employees only, many Lazarus customers never even knew of its existence. It was hidden away along with the corporate offices.

The cafeteria was designed to provide associates with good, inexpensive food. Among the favorite dishes were Swedish meatballs, refrigerated cheesecake and apple cheese crisp. Breakfasts were made to order. There was a snack bar, too, which was also strictly for employees. An unexpected benefit of the cafeteria was that it became a place where everyone, regardless of position in the store's hierarchy, got together to drink coffee and just hang out. "It was a family," Sue Robenalt says.

The Executive Dining Room, as the name implies, was used only by store management and their guests. It was the site of many "power" lunches, but it wasn't all business. Sometimes it hosted special events, such as luncheon for five physically disabled women from Creative Living.

The Pub at the Lazarus Café was located in the men's shoe department on the first floor. It was an approximation of an English pub, offering pizza, fish and chips, sandwiches and beer. As longtime Lazarus associate Jane Hostin noted, "We've got a wonderful little place tucked in here," catering

In 1950, the brand-new 1,500-seat Associates' Cafeteria was unveiled with its eighty-six-feet-long serving line. *PC.*

largely to state employees looking for a place to smoke. However, "It's not a happy-hour, after-work place." The Pub closed its doors on June 18, 1988.

Copper Kettle Lunch Counter, with its long counter that zigzagged back and forth across the room, was opened in the annex on February 28, 1957. It was known for its soups, including its namesake Copper Kettle vegetable soup, as well as shortcake and stuffed mushrooms. It also served burgers. Shillito's in Cincinnati operated a restaurant under this name.

The Highlander Grill (located in the West Basement, Front Street Level) replaced the soda grill during the early 1950s. Adjacent to the Budget Store, it served up such inexpensive items as breakfast, burgers, chili dogs and sandwiches. However, the Lazarus steamed celery dressing, nut bread and fruit betty were also available. During the later '50s and early '60s, a Lazburger was sold with a special sauce. This establishment closed on June 18, 1988.

A gourmet foods buffet was available in the Café on Five, located on the fifth floor. Opened in 1985, the restaurant featured Jane McDannold on the baby grand piano. Since the beginning, she had provided soothing music from 11:00 a.m. to 2:30 p.m., Monday through Saturdays, for those who stopped in for lunch. However, after thirteen years McDannold, sixty-seven, found herself without a job when Lazarus decided to discontinue the music.

Charles Lazarus was a visiting professor at Indiana University when he first met Iris Cooper in a marketing distribution class. Impressed with the young MBA student, he invited her to visit his store. Mr. Charles saw to it that Iris received the red carpet treatment, and she "fell in love with Columbus." Soon, she was plugged into the Lazarus buyer training program. After a brief stint in the bath shop, she was elevated to the position of marketing manager for the store's restaurants.

Iris was twenty-three, admittedly naïve and inexperienced in business, but Mr. Charles liked her inquisitiveness and enthusiasm. Serving as her mentor, he gave her the freedom to create or change the flagship store's restaurants however she saw fit. She approached the task the same way she would a case study in college.

During her tenure, Iris opened up three new restaurants and increased sales 10 percent. Studying the trends in nutrition, she decided to create Good For You, a health food bar, on the third floor close to ladies' clothing. It featured a circular salad bar, yogurt, fruit smoothies and other healthy fare.

In the annex, Iris opened the baseball-themed Home Plate, a meat and potatoes–style restaurant catering more to the blue-collar crowd. It was for those who were looking for traditional, home-cooked meals. She also opened

Subworks, a submarine sandwich shop. It was inspired by the Beatles' "Yellow Submarine" with its yellow-and-blue motif. This restaurant evolved into Charlie's.

Named after Mr. Charles, Charlie's bistro was located downstairs in the East Basement and was directly accessible by a stairway from Chapel Street. It focused on Italian fair, a fresh bar of vegetables and fruits and, of course, Charlie's submarine sandwich. Additional Charlie's restaurants were opened in the Eastland, Northland and Lafayette Mall stores, always in the basement. The menu included potato soup and the ever-popular "Hidden Sandwich."

While at Lazarus, Cooper worked with Don Charna and William "Bill" Williams. Williams later opened the popular Marble Gang Restaurant, featuring southern-style dishes. When he decided to produce a line of canned foods, he had Don and Iris assist him in testing the recipes. These three former Lazarus associates became the core of Glory Foods, which has developed into a multimillion-dollar company.

Iris left Lazarus in 1980 after three years. She explained that Federated was becoming more dictatorial, insisting that the restaurants in all their stores be the same across the board. This was in response to the rise of mall food courts and the increasing preference for fast foods. The classic "sit down and be waited on" restaurants were rapidly losing ground.

At the opposite end of the spectrum from Good For You was Waldo's Bakeshop, originally the Lazarus Bakery and Candy Counter. The shop was located in the downtown basement on the Front Street side and specialized in cookies (two for a dollar), baked cheesecake, fudge cake, macaroon tort, cake balls and similar treats. The concept was too good to restrict to one site and was soon expanded to the annex, Northland, Eastland and Westland.

In 1986, the "Grumpy Gourmet" described the two-hundred-seat Lazarus Food Court at the Northland store as "akin to a Roman orgy with a menu." In the basement, there were ten separate food stands, including the New York Deli, Waldo's Cookies, Charlie's Pizza, Delectable Desserts, Great Greens, Chicken Pickens, Crunchy Munchies, Federated Grill, Ice Cream Dreams and Philly Steak.

For a time, Pasta Cucina was an Italian restaurant adjacent to the Chintz Room. After it closed, it was converted into an English tearoom for one night only, with servers dressed as country maids. For this special occasion, the tea kettle whistled once again.

Located on the fifth floor, the Buckeye Room was known for its fast service. It also shared a kitchen with the Chintz Room. Among the entrees available at this establishment were Maryland-style chicken livers, carrot and apple scallop and chicken tetrazzini.

The Rose Fountain on the Front Street Level had some of the more adventurous (for the times) menu items, including the Lazarus Mexican beef sandwich, "peta pocket" and herb-seasoned green beans. The nearby Front Street Deli offered meats, imported cheeses, salads and breakfasts.

Between 1987 and 1998, Lazarus closed nine of its eleven remaining restaurants, many of them with little or no ceremony and few tears. Obviously, they were not being sufficiently patronized to keep them open. Some would say they weren't as good as they had once been.

Among the other restaurant names compiled by the columbuschefs.com website are Subworks (or, possibly, Sub Works, on the Front Street Level), Peasant Stock, Truffles Café, Coach Room and Flo's Café. The fact is that Lazarus tried out various concepts, some of which worked and became institutions, while others quickly disappeared from the pages of history.

The outlying stores had other restaurants in addition to the ones already mention. At Eastland, the Terrace Restaurant was on the second floor, overlooking the mall and toward the Sears store at the opposite end. It was here where Joe Sears once complained to a waitress that he didn't receive nearly as many potato chips with his cheeseburger platter as his friend had, only to be told that they were just for "decoration" anyway.

Because of its location along the old National Road, the Westland store's restaurant was called the Coach House and featured such comfort foods as chili, meatloaf and Ohio fruit delight salad. At one time, the Buckeye Room was located on the second floor of the Northland store and served up chicken scallop, Maryland fried turkey breast and that Columbus contribution to cafeteria cuisine: Johnny Marzetti.

At the Lima Mall, the in-house restaurant offered celery seed dressing, Hawaiian chicken salad and baked chicken salad. Diners at the Skyview Restaurant at Mansfield's Richland Mall could order sauerkraut salad, baked beans and Ozark pudding. Castleton, Indiana's Top of the Mall restaurant offered carrot cake, hot brown grill and quiche Lorraine.

In-store restaurants increasingly lost out to the mall's food courts. The food courts offered a wider selection of dining options and served up more quickly and, possibly, at a cheaper price. Most shoppers no longer cared about quality or aesthetics. More often than not, their kids decided where they would eat.

What follows are three of the most popular Lazarus restaurant recipes.

CHINTZ ROOM CHICKEN SALAD
(FROM *RECIPES FROM OUR KITCHEN*)

- *1 quart cooked chicken breasts, cubed 1½–2 inches*
- *1 quart celery, medium diced*
- *1 pint pecans, roasted and salted*
- *1 pint Lazarus Chicken Salad Dressing (see below)*

1. Mix chicken, celery and pecans together and add Lazarus Chicken Salad Dressing.
2. Toss gently. Do not over mix.

Lazarus Chicken Salad Dressing (from Recipes From Our Kitchen)

BOILED DRESSING

- *½ cup flour*
- *2 cups milk*
- *1 cup heated vinegar*
- *½ cup sugar*
- *2 teaspoons dry mustard*
- *1 tablespoon salt*
- *¼ cup egg yolks*
- *1 teaspoon paprika*

1. Thoroughly mix dry ingredients, add to milk and cook in a double boiler until flour is thoroughly cooked.
2. Add heated vinegar and continue to cook for ten minutes.
3. Beat egg yolks and add a little bit of the mixture to the yolks (to keep them from curdling); return the yolks to hot mixture and cook for ten minutes longer. Chill. Yields 1 quart.

MAYONNAISE

- *⅓ cup egg yolks*
- *4 teaspoons cider vinegar*

- *1 teaspoon salt*
- *1 tablespoon tarragon vinegar*
- *1 teaspoon paprika*
- *1 teaspoon Worcestershire sauce*
- *1 teaspoon dry mustard*
- *1 drop Tabasco sauce*
- *pinch white pepper*
- *1 tablespoon sugar*
- *4 teaspoons lemon juice*
- *3⅓ cups oil*

1. Combine dry ingredients with liquid ingredients, except oil and egg yolks.
2. Beat egg yolks until light and creamy.
3. Add vinegar mixture and oil alternately to beaten egg yolks, very slowly at first, until an emulsion is started.
4. Beat until a thick, creamy consistency.
5. Blend 1 part boiled dressing to 3 parts mayonnaise. Yield is for twelve large salads, or 1 quart.

Lazarus Bread Pudding With Whiskey Sauce (from *Recipes From Our Kitchen*)

Custard Mix

- *2 cups granulated sugar*
- *1 teaspoon salt*
- *8 extra-large eggs*
- *5½ cups milk*
- *1 teaspoon vanilla*

1. Blend eggs, salt and sugar lightly with wire whisk.
2. Add vanilla and milk. Blend and strain. Set aside.

Pudding

- *½ pound French bread, preferably stale*
- *¼ cup pecans, toasted*

- *4 ounces butter, melted*
- *custard mix (above)*

1. Break French bread into medium pieces.
2. Add pecans and melted butter.
3. Arrange in 9 x 13-inch baking dish.
4. Pour custard mix over bread pieces.
5. To bake, place the baking dish in a larger pan to create a double boiler effect.
6. Place a small amount of water in the bottom pan. Bake at 350 degrees for 50–60 minutes.
7. Test by inserting a knife blade into the center of the pudding.

WHISKEY SAUCE

- *8 ounces butter, melted*
- *2 cups powdered sugar*
- *2 extra-large eggs*
- *2 tablespoons whiskey*

1. Melt butter. Whip in powdered sugar.
2. Fold in eggs. Add whiskey.
3. Serve warm over bread pudding. Serves ten.

HIDDEN SANDWICH (FROM *RECIPES FROM OUR KITCHEN*)

- *1 slice rye bread*
- *1 ounce chicken (or turkey) breast, sliced*
- *1 ounce baked ham, sliced*
- *1 ounce Swiss cheese, sliced*
- *2 strips crisp bacon*
- *1 hard cooked egg, sliced*
- *2 tomato slices*
- *1 cup shredded lettuce*
- *½ cup Thousand Island (or Russian) dressing*

1. Place the baked ham, Swiss cheese and sliced chicken (or turkey) on the rye bread.

2. Mound the shredded lettuce on top.
3. Cover the sandwich with Thousand Island (or Russian) dressing and top with egg slices and tomato slices. Crisscross the strips of bacon.
4. Garnish with sweet pickle and carrot sticks (or cucumber slices).

This recipe has evolved slightly over the years, with turkey replacing the original chicken, cucumber slices edging out the carrot sticks, homemade Russian dressing instead of Thousand Island and the addition of bacon strips. Interestingly, the portions have also increased, from 1 tomato slice to 2 and ¼ cup of dressing to ½. Serves one.

Russian Dressing (from Recipes From Our Kitchen)

- *1 quart Hellmann's mayonnaise*
- *2 tablespoons onion, grated*
- *2 tablespoons green pepper, chopped*
- *½ cup chili sauce*
- *½ teaspoon Worcestershire sauce*
- *⅛ teaspoon red wine vinegar*
- *1 teaspoon salt*
- *1 tablespoon sweet relish*

1. Combine all ingredients and blend well. Refrigerate. Yield approximately 5 cups.

Appendix III

La Belle Pomme

In 1973, Betty Griffin Rosbottom found herself in Columbus by a rather circuitous route. "I was in my early thirties," she told Nancy Miller Lewis, "and didn't know what to do. But I knew whatever I did, I had to love it, and it also had to be something I could do the rest of my life."

A southern belle by birth, Betty had two consuming passions: art and food. So while working at the Columbus Museum of Art, she taught cooking classes on the side for her own enjoyment. Encouraged by her friends in the art world, she decided to open a formal cooking school.

Before coming to Ohio, Betty had studied cuisine in New Orleans, Philadelphia and Paris. Along the way, she had also taken a course in operating a small business. As she recounted for Tricia Wheeler, she had gone to Paris as a young college student and fell in love with the food. So when her husband gave her Julia Child's *Mastering the Art of French Cooking*, volume 1, as a wedding present, she proceeded to cook her way through it.

Curious as to whether others in the community shared her interest in the culinary arts, Betty placed "a small, unassuming advertisement in the weekly *Upper Arlington News*. Buried between the garage sales and the used-furniture ads, mine was easy to miss, but one woman saw it and called to inquire about classes. She signed up not only herself, but three other friends as well."

Initially, Betty gave cooking classes in her home, but in 1976 she took out a loan to lease a five-hundred-square-feet space in Northwest Gardens. "I knew it had to have a great name, and I loved New York, but the Big Apple doesn't translate well in French, so I decided to call it the Beautiful Apple"—La Belle Pomme.

Betty Rosbottom almost single-handedly put Columbus on the culinary map with her La Belle Pomme Cooking School. *PC.*

Although she was terrified that no one would show up, the response was overwhelming. Located at the corner of Northwest Boulevard and North Star Road, La Belle Pomme started modestly with a handful of students, offering such courses as Winner Soups, A Riviera Cookout, Favorites from the French Bakery, Summer Buffets and Kids Are Cooks Too! Betty also led groups of her students on weeklong working pilgrimages to Paris.

From the beginning, Betty had bigger plans but kept them under wraps for about a year. Then she brought Jacques Pepin, author of *La Technique* and one-time chef to Charles de Gaulle, to her school for a three-day course. She followed up with Marcella Hazan, the foremost exponent of Italian cooking, and Maida Heatter, the dessert queen, who became a good friend. Their classes sold out immediately.

However, what really put La Belle Pomme on the culinary map was a 1979 article in *Time* magazine. By a fortunate stroke of serendipity, writer Michael Demarest chose her school as the focus of a story on how a cooking craze was sweeping the country. After the piece was published, Betty found herself suddenly deluged with letters from all over the world.

Not surprisingly, Betty's little school began to develop a big reputation. Within the year, she was asked by the *Columbus Dispatch* to contribute a weekly cooking column to the paper, "For the Gourmet." Two years afterward, her school was acquired by F&R Lazarus & Company and relocated to the fifth floor of the downtown store.

The advantages of this arrangement were enormous. For one, the school was already at capacity, so it would have had to move to a new location anyway. For another, Lazarus had the resources to expand it even more. But the key to the relationship was the fact that Lazarus did not ask Betty to compromise her high standards.

Betty was now ready to publish her first cookbook, *Betty Rosbottom's Cooking School Cookbook* (Workman Publishing, 1987). Many others have followed. One of her recipes calls for sun-dried cherries, which, to her amusement, the food editors of California-based *Bon Appétit* did not have in their test kitchen. Not surprisingly, the magazine's editors have also become her fans.

So many people took classes at La Belle Pomme that students began to recognize Betty's menus when they attended dinner parties at the homes of friends—even friends who had not taken lessons at her school.

Praising Betty's contribution to local cuisine, one of her instructors observed that "the school has sharpened tastes and palates in town. They needed to be sharpened." However, a number of her students weren't exactly novices, having previously attended other famous cooking schools, both in the United States and abroad.

One of Betty's favorite memories involved Pepin. "His classes were so popular and sold out so quickly that to get in was a big deal. One woman who was planning to come had a major emergency at her home the morning of one of Jacques's classes, and…she called a friend to give away her place in the 'Jacques Pepin' course before dialing 911."

Betty's school became nationally acclaimed and probably would have continued until Lazarus shut its doors. But as the wife of Ronald Rosbottom, chairman of Romance languages at Ohio State University, she was faced with a dilemma when her husband accepted a job at Amherst College in 1989.

Unwilling to abandon her school, Betty spent the next six years commuting between Ohio and Massachusetts, spending her weekdays at La Belle Pomme and her weekends with her family. At its peak, she and a staff of ten were conducting one hundred classes per year. However, she finally gave up this "insane arrangement" in 1995.

Since leaving Columbus, Betty has served as cooking school coordinator for Different Drummer's Kitchen in Northampton, Massachusetts. She also writes a syndicated column, "That's Entertaining!" and hosts a PBS television show, *On the Menu*, for WGBY. Both NBC's *Today Show* and CBS's *The Early Show* have had her on as a guest.

Betty recalled for Tricia Wheeler the most memorable dishes she taught at La Belle Pomme: "A mushroom pâté, which I still make to this day; barbecued shrimp in their shells, a recipe that has appeared in more than one of my cookbooks; and the chocolate ribbon cake, which was on the cover of *Bon Appétit* in 1984." These three recipes have been reprinted (below) courtesy of Ms. Rosbottom and *Bon Appétit*.

MUSHROOM PÂTÈ
(FROM *BETTY ROSBOTTOM'S COOKING SCHOOL COOKBOOK*)

Betty said that her students preferred this appetizer to any other she prepared in her classes, both because it was so easy to make and because it tastes delicious. She suggested that Belgian endive leaves can be substitute for toast points.

- *4 tablespoons (½ stick) unsalted butter, at room temperature*
- *8 ounces mushrooms, cleaned and finely chopped*
- *1½ teaspoons garlic, finely chopped*
- *¼ cup finely chopped scallions (green onions), white parts only*
- *⅓ cup homemade chicken stock or good-quality canned broth*
- *4 ounces cream cheese, at room temperature*
- *3 tablespoons finely minced fresh chives or green scallion tops*
- *salt and freshly ground pepper to taste*
- *1 teaspoon chopped chives or green tops of scallions, for garnish*
- *toast points*

1. Melt 2 tablespoons of the butter in a medium-sized skillet over high heat. When it is hot, add the chopped mushrooms and sauté 2 to 3 minutes. Add the garlic and the scallions and sauté 1 minute more. Add the chicken stock and cook over high heat until all liquid has evaporated, 4 to 5 minutes. Let the mushroom mixture cool to room temperature.

La Belle Pomme

2. Combine the cream cheese and the remaining 2 tablespoons butter in a mixing bowl and stir to mix well. Add the mushroom mixture, minced chives and salt and pepper. Mix well. Fill a 1-cup crockery bowl or an individual ramekin or soufflé dish with the mushroom mixture. Cover with plastic wrap and refrigerate until needed. (The pate can be made a day in advance to this point.)
3. When ready to serve, sprinkle the pate with chopped chives and garnish with toast points. Serves 6.

CREOLE BARBECUED SHRIMP
(FROM *BETTY ROSBOTTOM'S COOKING SCHOOL COOKBOOK*)

According to Betty, her husband requests this dish every year for his birthday. She serves it with fresh buttered green beans, caraway potato salad and, for dessert, crème caramel.

- 18 scallions (green onions)
- 1 cup (2 sticks) unsalted butter
- 12 cloves garlic, chopped
- 1⅓ cups dry white wine
- 2 tablespoons plus 1 teaspoon fresh lemon juice
- freshly ground pepper to taste
- 36 large shrimp in the shell, legs removed
- 1 cup chopped fresh parsley
- hot pepper sauce to taste
- salt to taste
- lemon wedges
- 2 tablespoons minced fresh parsley, for garnish
- 2 tablespoons minced scallions (green onions), for garnish
- 2 tablespoons chopped fresh chives, for garnish

1. Chop the scallions, including 2 inches of the green stems. Melt the butter in a heavy Dutch oven or deep casserole (not aluminum) over medium-low heat. Add the scallions and garlic and cook, stirring, for 3 minutes. Add the wine and simmer for 15 minutes.
2. Remove the pan from the heat and stir in the lemon juice and a generous amount of pepper. Set aside to cool to room temperature.

3. Using a paring knife, cut the shrimp down the back of the devein but do not peel. Toss the shrimp and the 1 cup of parsley in the scallion mixture. Refrigerate, covered, 6 hours or overnight, turning occasionally.
4. Prepare a charcoal grill. When the coals are hot, add the hickory chunks and heat them until the wood smokes, about 15 minutes.
5. Meanwhile, remove the shrimp from the marinade. Heat the marinade in a medium-size heavy saucepan. Strain and return it to the pan. Cook over medium-heat until reduced by half, 5 to 10 minutes. Add the hot pepper sauce and salt to taste. Cover the sauce and keep it warm.
6. Place the shrimp on the grill and cook until they curl up and turn pink, 5 to 6 minutes. Turn once during the grilling time. Do not overcook, or the shrimp will become tough and the shells will be hard to remove.
7. Mound the shrimp on a warm serving platter. Garnish with lemon wedges. Pour the sauce into individual ramekins or a serving bowl. Sprinkle the minced parsley, scallions and chives over the sauce. Serve the shrimp and dipping sauce immediately. Serves 6.

CHOCOLATE RIBBON CAKE (FROM *BON APPÉTIT* AND *BETTY ROSBOTTOM'S COOKING SCHOOL COOKBOOK*)

More than twenty-six years after Betty's show-stopping ribbon cake appeared on the cover of *Bon Appétit* in December 1984, it remains the magazine's most requested recipe. As the magazine's website puts it: "Want to know what all the fuss is about? It's about chocolate-spice layers, chocolate-rum buttercream filling, and honey-sweetened bittersweet chocolate glaze—plus it looks like a giant holiday present." It also made Betty justifiably famous.

Special equipment: three straight-sided 9-inch round cake pans; heavy-duty electric mixer.

CAKE

*   *1½ cups (3 sticks) butter, at room temperature*
*   *2 cups sugar*
*   *8 large eggs, separated, at room temperature*
*   *10 ounces semisweet chocolate, melted*
*   *1½ cups finely chopped pecans*
*   *2 teaspoons vanilla extract*

- *1 teaspoon ground cinnamon*
- *1 teaspoon ground cloves*
- *1 teaspoon freshly grated nutmeg*
- *1⅓ cups all purpose flour, sifted*
- *pinch of salt*
- *pinch of cream of tartar*

BUTTERCREAM

- *¾ cup sugar*
- *½ cup light corn syrup*
- *4 jumbo egg yolks*
- *1½ cups (3 sticks) unsalted butter, cut into small pieces, at room temperature*
- *6 ounces semisweet chocolate, melted and cooled*
- *¼ cup dark rum*

GLAZE

- *12 ounces semisweet chocolate, broken into small pieces*
- *¾ cup (1½ sticks) unsalted butter, cut into small pieces*
- *2 tablespoons honey*
- *¾ teaspoon instant coffee powder*

GARNISH: *WHITE AND DARK CHOCOLATE RIBBONS*

1. Position a rack in center of the oven, and preheat to 350°F.
2. Prepare the cake: Butter and flour three 9-inch-diameter cake pans. Line the bottom of each with waxed paper; butter and flour the paper.
3. Cream the butter in the large bowl of a heavy-duty electric mixer. Gradually beat in the sugar until smooth. Beat in the egg yolks, one at a time. Blend in the melted chocolate. Slowly mix in the pecans, vanilla and spices. Gently fold in the flour in four batches (the batter will be very thick and dense).
4. Using an electric mixer, beat the egg whites with salt and cream of tartar until medium peaks form. Gently fold one fourth of the whites into the batter to lighten it and then fold in the remaining whites. Divide the batter among the prepared cake pans, spreading it evenly.

5. Bake the cake layers until a toothpick inserted in the center comes out clean, 35 to 40 minutes. Run a knife around the edge of each cake. Let them stand 10 minutes and then invert the cakes onto racks. Cool to room temperature. (The cake layers can be prepared two weeks ahead. Wrap then tightly in plastic wrap and then aluminum foil, and freeze. Bring to room temperature before using. It will take about 24 hours to thaw in the refrigerator.)

6. Prepare the buttercream: Stir the sugar and corn syrup in medium-size heavy saucepan over medium heat until the mixture boils. Cook 1 minute and remove from heat.

7. Beat the egg yolks with an electric mixer on medium speed until they are pale and thick. Gradually beat in the hot sugar syrup and continue beating until the mixture is completely cool, about 5 minutes.

8. Beat in butter one piece at a time, incorporating each piece completely before adding the next. Blend in the chocolate and then the rum. (The buttercream can be made 2 days ahead; cover with plastic wrap and refrigerate. Let stand at room temperature to soften before spreading, 30 minutes to 1 hour.)

9. Set aside ½ cup of the buttercream. Set one cake layer, flat side up, on a rack. Spread it with half of the remaining buttercream. Top with the second cake layer (flat side up) and spread it with the remaining buttercream. Top with the third cake layer (flat side up). Use the reserved ½ cup of buttercream to fill in the "seams" where the layers meet. Wrap the cake loosely in foil and freeze cake until the buttercream is firm, about 2 hours.

10. Prepare the glaze: Stir the chocolate, butter, honey and coffee powder together in the top of a double boiler over gently simmering water. Cook until the mixture is smooth and shiny, 4 to 5 minutes. Remove the pan from the heat and stir until the glaze is thickened, about 5 minutes; do not allow to set.

11. Pour three quarters of the glaze over the top of the cake. Carefully and quickly tilt the cake back and forth so the glaze coats the sides. Smooth the sides with spatula, adding some of the remaining glaze where necessary. Refrigerate the cake until the glaze is set, 2 hours or longer. (The cake can be glazed 1 to 2 days in advance. Cover it with plastic wrap and aluminum foil after the glaze is set. The cake can be frozen; bring to a refrigerator temperature before using. It will take about 24 hours to thaw in the refrigerator.) Decorate the cake with the ribbons. Serves 12 to 14.

White and Dark Chocolate Ribbons
(from *Bon Appétit* and *Betty Rosbottom's Cooking School Cookbook*)

Special equipment: pasta machine; rimless baking sheet.

- *7 ounces white chocolate, broken into pieces*
- *½ cup light corn syrup*
- *7 ounces semisweet chocolate, broken into pieces*

1. Melt the white chocolate in the top of double boiler over gently simmering water; stir until smooth. Stir in ¼ cup of the syrup. Pour the mixture onto a rimmed baking sheet and refrigerate until firm, 30 to 40 minutes.
2. Transfer the white chocolate to work surface and knead it until it is pliable, 3 to 4 minutes. Shape it into a ball, wrap in plastic wrap and let it stand at room temperature for 1 hour.
3. Repeat with the semisweet chocolate.
4. Cut the white chocolate into four pieces. Flatten one piece into rectangle. Turn a pasta machine to its widest setting and run the chocolate through three times, folding it into thirds before each run.
5. Adjust the machine to the next narrower setting. Run chocolate through the machine without folding. If the chocolate is more than $1/16$-inch thick, run it through the next narrower setting. Lay that piece on a rimless baking sheet. Repeat the flattening, folding and rolling with the remaining pieces.
6. Repeat process with semisweet chocolate.
7. Cut four 8 x 1-inch strips from the white chocolate and four 8 x ½-inch strips from the semisweet chocolate. Center the dark chocolate strips on the white chocolate strips to form four ribbons. Run one ribbon from base of the cake to the center. Arrange remaining three equidistant from one another in same fashion.
8. Cut ten 6½ x 1-inch strips from the white chocolate dough and ten 6½ x ½-inch strips from the semisweet chocolate. Center the dark chocolate strips on the white chocolate strips to form ten ribbons.
9. Cut the ends off two ribbons on the diagonal. Starting at the center, drape the ribbons over the top and sides of the cake to form "trailers." Fold the remaining eight ribbons in half, layered side out.

Cut the ends into V shapes. Arrange the ribbon halves with the V shapes at the center of the cake to form a bow.

10. Cut one 3 x 1-inch strip of white chocolate and one 3 x ½-inch strip of semisweet chocolate. Center the dark chocolate strip on the white chocolate strip. Fold in ends and pinch to resemble a knot and then place it in the center of the bow. Transfer the cake to a platter. (The ribbons can be prepared 1 day ahead and refrigerated. The cake with the ribbons can also be wrapped in plastic wrap and then with foil and frozen for several weeks. Thaw the cake in the refrigerator for 24 hours and then bring it to room temperature before serving.)

Appendix IV

A Gamut of Retail Options

This directory of the flagship Lazarus store is adapted from a terrific blog: the Department Store Museum (http://departmentstoremuseum. blogspot.com). BAK, the blogger, asks the question, "Why are we not good enough for such a gamut of retail options today?"

F&R LAZARUS & COMPANY
141 South High Street
Columbus, Ohio 43215

ANNEX LOWER LEVEL
The Copper Kettle • Sporting Goods • Sporting Goods Apparel • Sport Shoes • Paint Center • Home Improvement • Hard Surface Coverings

ANNEX MAIN FLOOR
Camera • Luggage • Sewing Center • Casual Living • Bath Shop • Housewares • Tabletop • Floor Care • Cleaning Supplies • Small Electrics • Major Appliances • Cookware • Unfinished Furniture • Fireplace Shop • Hardware • Office Supplies • Garden Shop

EAST BASEMENT
Charlie's • Lazarus Basement Budget Store (Women's Store)

WEST BASEMENT
Highlander Grill • Lazarus Basement Budget Store (Men's and Children's Store)

FRONT STREET LEVEL
Television • Stereo • Records • The Rose Fountain

FIRST FLOOR
Fine Jewelry • Fashion Jewelry • Precious Metals • Little Shop • Accessories • Rainwear • Handbags • Small Leather Goods • Gloves • Hosiery • Handkerchiefs • Tovar Wig Bar • Millinery • First Floor Sportswear • Blouses • Sweaters • Accessory Tops • Cosmetics • Candy • Stationery • Calculators and Office Equipment • Books • Notions • Drugs • The Colonial Room • Men's Accessories • Men's Furnishing • Men's Handkerchiefs • Men's Shirts • Men's Ties • Men's Sports Furnishings • First-Floor Men's Sportswear • First-Floor Men's Slacks and Sport Coats

SECOND FLOOR
Women's Shoes • Headgear • Sound Stage II • Misses' Sportswear • Women's Sportswear • Women's Dresses • Career Shop • Uniforms • Sleepwear • Daywear • Foundations • Beauty Salon • Men's Clothing • Men's Outerwear • Men's Shoes • Men's Hats • Men's Designer Shop • Via Europa • Town Shop • University Shop • Big and Tall Men's Shop • Men's Better Sportswear • Men's Contemporary Shop • Men's Loungewear

THIRD FLOOR
Collegienne Dresses • Collegienne Sportswear • Collegienne Coats • Collegienne Shoes • Junior Sport • Misses' Dresses • Cosmopolitan Shop • Better Dresses • Better Sportswear • Better Women's Dresses • Discovery Sportswear • Town and Country Dresses • Discovery Dresses • Point of View • Coat Salon • Suit Salon • Fur Salon • Bridal Salon • Carriage House • Accessory Bars • Designer Dresses • Designer Sportswear • The Club House • Collector's Choice • The Wedgewood Room • Shoe Salon • The Shop for Pappagallo • The Aigner Collection • Daywear-Lingerie • Underscene • Bras and Girdles • Robes • Sleepwear • Jr. Lingerie

FOURTH FLOOR
Decorator Furniture • Occasional Furniture • Modern Furniture • Traditional Furniture • Early American Furniture • Sleep Shop • Bedroom Furniture • Dining Room Furniture • Modern Dinettes • Floor Coverings • Rugs • Draperies • Decorator Fabrics • Driver Training Center

FIFTH FLOOR

Music Center • Linens • Bedding • Fabrics • Art Needlework • China • Glassware • Silver • Gifts • Lamps • Pictures, Mirrors • Home Accessories • Guest Lounge • The Chintz Room • The Buckeye Room

SIXTH FLOOR

Boys 1–6 • Boys 6–16 • The Body Shop • Children's Furniture • Teen Center • Girls 7–14 • Little Girls 3–6x • Girls' Sleepwear • Girls' Accessories • Infants' Wear • Toddlers' Wear • Infants' Furniture • Toys • Adult Games • Portrait Studio • Watch and Jewelry Repair • Assembly Room

CIVIC CENTER DRIVE AND RICH STREET

Auto Service Center

Notes

CHAPTER 1

1. David Copperfield, in the Charles Dickens novel of the same name, visits a slop shop to sell his jacket.
2. An arsonist destroyed the "old" statehouse early in 1852, most likely to force the issue of the new one's completion.
3. The Central Market served the same functions that the ancient Greek "Agora" had as a place both to "speak" and to "shop."
4. She lived at 165 Goodale Street, on the northern edge of "Flytown," one of the city's least affluent neighborhoods.

CHAPTER 2

5. Coincidentally, 1851 was also the year when Aristide Boucicaut opened Le Bon Marche ("The Good Market"), considered by many to be the world's first department store.
6. Another version of the story has Morgan himself stealing clothes from the store following his escape from the Ohio Penitentiary, but this seems less likely.
7. From the Many Happy Returns to Lazarus website, www.wosu.org/archive/Lazarus.

CHAPTER 3

8. Sidney Cohen, Abe's son, was a notorious gambler who became silent film star Roscoe "Fatty" Arbuckle's manager.

CHAPTER 4

9. Promoted by Mayor George J. Karb, Columbus became widely known as the "Arch City" until they were all torn down in 1914.
10. Selfridge is also credited with the immortal "Only [blank] Shopping Days Until Christmas!"

CHAPTER 5

11. Charles Dana Gibson's drawings of beautiful, independent young women were extremely popular before World War I.
12. A "glide" was a popular dance step of the period.
13. At the Boston Store, owned by the Hirsch Kobacker and sons, out-of-town shoppers were encouraged to write to the equally imaginary "Susan Sharp."

CHAPTER 6

14. From Bernstein, *Thurber: A Biography*.

CHAPTER 7

15. This incident was described by her son, Luke Yankee, in his book *Just Outside the Spotlight*.
16. From Ross and Ross, *The Player*.

CHAPTER 8

17. From Buck, *"That's a Winner!"*
18. The term "escalator" had been trademarked by the Otis Elevator Corporation.

Chapter 9

19. One of the chaplains, Clark V. Poling, was from Columbus. As a child, this diorama was attorney David Korn's favorite.
20. From Garrett, *Columbus*.
21. From Greene, *Fifty Year Dash*.

Appendix I

22. According to one Cincinnati financial writer, the atmosphere at the Federated headquarters was one of "pouncing alertness."
23. The new Lazarus Bulk Service Building was an example of how the old ways of doing things could be improved.
24. From Kelly, *Trouble Is Not in Your Set*.

Bibliography

Newspapers

Columbus Citizen.
Columbus Citizen-Journal.
Columbus Dispatch.
Ohio State Journal.

Books and Articles

Bach, Sarah Mills, and Marshall Hood. "The Union to Close in '94: 'Last Of Carriage-Trade' Merchants 99 Years Old." *Columbus Dispatch*, November 10, 1993.

Bernstein, Burton. *Thurber: A Biography*. New York: William Morrow & Company, 1996.

Bosworth, Adrienne. "Lazarus, the Store: The Decline of a Great Institution." *Columbus Monthly*, May 1990.

Buck, Jack. *"That's a Winner!"* Champaign, IL: Sports Publishing LLC, 2002.

Cohen, I. David. *Sorry, Downtown Columbus Is Closed.* Columbus, OH: I.D. Cohen, 2009.

Cook, Herb, Jr. "Lazarus, the Family: The End of a Dynasty." *Columbus Monthly*, May 1990.

Demarest, Michael. "In Ohio: Saut," *Time*, May 21, 1979.

Garrett, Betty. *Columbus: America's Crossroads*. Tulsa, OK: Continental Heritage Press 1980.

Greene, Bob. *The Fifty Year Dash*. New York: Doubleday & Company, 1997.

Hambrick, Jennifer. "A Year Without Lazarus." *Short North Gazette*, August 2005.

Hendrickson, Robert. *The Grand Emporiums*. New York: Stein and Day, 1979.

Hunker, Henry L. *Columbus, Ohio: A Personal Geography*. Columbus: Ohio State University Press, 2000.

Kaplan, Peggy. "Interview with Herb Topy (Topolosky)." *Columbus Jewish Historical Society Oral History Project*, February 26, 2007.

Kelly, Mary Ann. *The Trouble Is Not in Your Set*. Cincinnati, OH: C.J. Krehbiel Company, 1990.

Kiplinger magazine. "Retailing Is Like Baby's Milk," March 1947.

Lazarus, Fred, Jr. *Up from the Family Store.* New York: Newcomen Society in North America, 1957.

Lee, Alfred E. *History of the City of Columbus, Capital of Ohio*. Vols. 1–2. New York: W.W. Munsell & Company, 1892.

Lewis, Nancy Miller. "An Apple for the Teacher." *More Columbus Unforgettables*. Columbus, OH: Robert D. Thomas, 1986.

McGill, Mary Robinson. *You and Your Friends.* Columbus, OH: F.J. Heer Printing Company, 1906.

McKay, Robert. "Taking Federated." *Cincinnati* magazine, April 1988.

McKelvey, Blake. "The Men's Clothing Industry in Rochester's History." *Rochester History*, July 1960.

Meyers, David, and Elise Meyers. *Central Ohio's Historic Prisons.* Charleston, SC: Arcadia Publishing, 2009.

Miller, Stephen. "Charles Y. Lazarus (1914–2007): The Last of Four Generations to Run Iconic Columbus, Ohio, Department Store." *Wall Street Journal*, May 19, 2007.

Raphael, Marc Lee. "The Early Jews of Columbus, Ohio: A Study in Economic Mobility, 1850–1880." *American Jewish History*. New York: Routledge, 1998.

———. *Jews and Judaism in a Midwestern Community: Columbus, Ohio, 1840–1975.* Columbus: Ohio Historical Society, 1979.

Rosbottom, Betty. *Betty Rosbottom's Cooking School Cookbook.* New York: Workman Publishing Company, 1987.

Ross, Lillian, and Helen Ross. *The Player: The Profile of an Art.* New York: Simon & Schuster, 1962.

Rothschild, John. *Going for Broke.* New York: Simon & Schuster, 1991.

Schwartz, Jonathan L. *A Store Refashioned: The Changing Face of the F. & R. Lazarus Company.* Princeton, NJ: Princeton University, 1999.

Shkolnik, Carol. "Interview With Don Levy." *Columbus Jewish Historical Society Oral History Project*, November 11, 1996.

Soucek, Gayle. *Marshall Field's: The Store that Helped Build Chicago.* Charleston, SC: The History Press, 2010.

Strege, Gayle. *Capital Fashion: 1851–1965.* Columbus: Ohio State University, 2003.

———. "Influences of Two Midwestern American Department Stores on Retailing Practices, 1883–1941." *Business and Economic History On-Line.* Vol. 7, 2009.

Turner, Tracy. "The End's in Sight—Schottenstein's Original Store on Parsons Avenue to Close." *Columbus Dispatch,* January 7, 2

Wheeler, Tricia. "Catching Up With Culinary Icon Betty Rosbottom." Edible Columbus, ediblecommunities.com, spring 2010.

Whittaker, Jan. *Service and Style: How the American Department Store Fashioned the Middle Class.* New York: St. Martin's Press, 2006.

———. *Tea at the Blue Lantern Inn: A Social History of the Tea Room Craze in America.* New York: St. Martin's Press, 2002.

Willson, Brad. "The Lazarus Store." *Columbus Sunday Dispatch Magazine,* February 4, 1951.

WOSU-TV. "Many Happy Returns to Lazarus." http://www.wosu.org/archive/lazarus/index.php.

Yankee, Luke. *Just Outside the Spotlight: Growing Up with Eileen Heckart.* New York: Back Stage Books, 2006.

Yerian, Mari C. "Fred Lazarus Sr. and Sons." *Columbus Unforgettables.* Columbus, OH: Robert D. Thomas, 1983.

Yerian, Mari C. (uncredited). *Lazarus: Established 1851.* Columbus, OH: F&R Lazarus & Company, 1978.

Young, Betty. "Interview With Charles Lazarus." *Columbus Jewish Historical Society Oral History Project,* November 12, 1995. http://www.columbusjewishhistoricalsociety.org/oral_histories/index.html.

About the Authors

The family that shops together doesn't necessarily write together, but the Meyers family felt it was the best way to tackle a book about Lazarus. After all, the story of the renowned department store was their story, too (the shopping part, anyway).

David holds degrees from Miami University and Ohio State University, where his wife, Beverly, obtained a BS in art education. Elise, their daughter, earned a BA in art history from Hofstra University.

After a thirty-year career in corrections, David now works at Columbus State Community College. Besides stints as a teacher and event planner, Beverly was a professional puppeteer and handled publicity for the Big Apple Circus. Elise has been a freelance magazine writer, a performer at Disney World and a member of a professional theater company in New York. She is also employed at Columbus State.

David and Elise previously collaborated on *Central Ohio's Historic Prisons* (Arcadia, 2009) and *Historic Columbus Crimes: Mama's in the Furnace, The Thing & More* (The History Press, 2010).

Visit us at
www.historypress.net